teaching
information literacy
50 Standards-Based Exercises for College Students

Second Edition

Joanna M. Burkhardt
Mary C. MacDonald

with Andrée J. Rathemacher

American Library Association
Chicago   2010

Joanna M. Burkhardt is professor and head librarian at the University of Rhode Island (URI) branch libraries in Providence and Narragansett. She coordinates the information literacy program at the branches and teaches sections of URI's course in information literacy. She also serves as the chair of technical services for the university libraries. She is an active member of the American Library Association (ALA), the Association of College and Research Libraries (ACRL), and the Rhode Island Library Association.

Mary C. MacDonald is an associate professor and head of instructional services in the library at the University of Rhode Island, Kingston. She teaches sections of URI's course in information literacy. She is an active member of ALA, ACRL, and the Rhode Island Library Association, and she is a member of the ACRL Institute for Information Literacy's Immersion Program faculty.

Andrée J. Rathemacher is an associate professor and head of acquisitions in the library at the University of Rhode Island, Kingston. She has taught in the library's information literacy program and has designed information literacy modules that have been integrated into the university curriculum. She is an active member of the ALA, ACRL, and NASIG (North American Serials Interest Group).

The authors were winners of the Outstanding Paper of the Year in *Reference Services Review* for the year 2000: "Challenges in Building an Incremental, Multiyear Information Literacy Plan," *RSR: Reference Services Review* 28, no. 3 (2000): 240–247.

ISBN-13: 978-0-8389-1053-5

Printed in the United States of America
14 13 12   5 4 3

While extensive effort has gone into ensuring the reliability of information appearing in this book, the publisher makes no warranty, express or implied, with respect to the material contained herein.

Library of Congress Cataloging-in-Publication Data
Burkhardt, Joanna M.
    Teaching information literacy : 50 standards-based exercises for college students /
Joanna M. Burkhardt and Mary C. MacDonald with Andrée J. Rathemacher. — 2nd ed.
        p.   cm.
    Includes bibliographical references and index.
    ISBN 978-0-8389-1053-5 (alk. paper)
    1. Information literacy—Study and teaching (Higher) 2. Information resources—Evaluation—Study and teaching (Higher) 3. Research—Methodology—Study and teaching (Higher) 4. Electronic information resource literacy—Study and teaching (Higher) 5. Computer network resources—Evaluation—Study and teaching (Higher) 6. Internet research—Study and teaching (Higher) 7. Library orientation for college students. I. MacDonald, Mary C. II. Rathemacher, Andrée J. III. Title.
ZA3075.B87 2010
028.7071'1—dc22
                                                                                    2009045780

Book design in Caecilia and Electra by Casey Bayer.

♾ This paper meets the requirements of ANSI/NISO Z39.48-1992 (Permanence of Paper).

ALA Editions also publishes its books in a variety of electronic formats.
For more information, visit the ALA Store at www.alastore.ala.org and select eEditions.

Contents

Exercises

Preface

Since the first edition of this book was published, in 2003, the world has continued on its path toward digitization and electronic communication. More types of all electronic sources are available every day. Wikis, blogs, RSS feeds, twittering, Google Books, collaborative writing tools, and many other new devices have added to the means by which information is available. Unfortunately, problems surrounding the identification, selection, evaluation, and use of information have not changed substantially. We still find that although many traditional students know how to use technology, they do not know how to make the best use of the information they find. They do not know how to separate the good from the bad, the weak from the strong, the real from the imaginary. These students need training in information literacy, that is, training that allows them to

- determine the extent of information needed;
- access the needed information effectively and efficiently;
- evaluate information and its sources critically;
- incorporate selected information into one's knowledge base;
- use information effectively to accomplish a specific purpose; and
- understand the economic, legal, and social issues surrounding the use of information, and access and use information ethically and legally (for more information, see the ACRL standards website, at www.ala .org/ala/mgrps/divs/acrl/standards/informationliteracycompetency .cfm#ildef).

In addition, many more nontraditional students are appearing in classrooms, some with not-so-up-to-date technological skills. These students require information literacy training as well.

During the years since the first edition of this book was published, our experience has broadened and our knowledge has deepened. We have incorporated the knowledge and expertise of the colleagues who have joined our instruction program. We have benefited from the best practices noted in the literature and shared by our colleagues all over the world. Our methods have developed to make our teaching more student-centered and the learning process more problem-based and active. We have attempted to make learning about information literacy more about student discovery and less about instructor delivery.

In this edition we have added several chapters to generally explain how new technology can be incorporated into teaching information literacy. Most chapters have new or updated exercises or both. We invited several colleagues who teach the Library 120 course, Introduction to Information Literacy, at the University of Rhode Island (URI) to share their expertise through chapters and exercises. These contributors include Kate Cheromcha, Amanda K. Izenstark, Jim Kinnie, and Peter J. Larsen. We have also included exercises based on original work by Barbara F. Kenney, of Roger Williams University in Bristol, Rhode Island; by Libby Miles, of the University of Rhode Island; and by a former University of Rhode Island GSLIS student, Carrie A. Kelly, who is currently the librarian at St. George's School in Newport, Rhode Island. All of these individuals have made our teaching experience richer by sharing their creative ideas about how to approach and deliver content in their fields of expertise. By sharing some of these ideas in the second edition of this book, we hope to pass on some of this creativity and to make their tested practices and exercises available to a larger audience.

Although the ACRL "Information Literacy Competency Standards for Higher Education, Standards, Performance Indicators, and Outcomes," published in 2000, remain unchanged, several ALA subject-specialty groups have used the standards to craft standards that are specific to their disciplines: "Political Science Research Competency Guidelines" (July 2008); "Information Literacy Standards for Anthropology and Sociology Students" (January 2008); "Research Competency Guidelines for Literatures in English" (June 2007); and "Information Literacy Standards for Science and Engineering/Technology" (June 2006). These standards have been vetted by ACRL and appear under "Standards and Guidelines" at the ACRL website (www.ala.org/ala/mgrps/divs/acrl/stan dards/index.cfm).

ACKNOWLEDGMENTS

We would like to acknowledge the assistance of our families, colleagues, students, employers, and editors in the preparation of this manuscript. We are especially grateful for the patience and forbearance of all of those who helped us through the process, critiqued our exercises, listened to our discussions, read our drafts, and "stood in" for us at events and occasions while we were writing.

Introduction

Research on how people learn has been going on for decades. It has been found that each person brings different strengths, skills, and experiences to a learning opportunity. Whether they learn anything depends largely upon the individual. The instructor can present material in any number of ways, but it is possible that none of these methods will be useful to everyone in a group of learners. Some students prefer verbal presentations, others respond better to visuals, and still others excel only when they can try something themselves (hands-on). No one method can reach every student. An instructor who wants students to succeed must try to incorporate as many learning methods as possible into his or her teaching sessions or must vary his or her presentation so that all students will have success in some part of the learning experience. There is some evidence that the combination of hearing a verbal explanation and doing a hands-on example relating to the explanation creates a learning situation in which the majority of students learn and retain the lesson.

Students today take a very different approach to research than did their counterparts of twenty or even ten years ago. Gone are the days of the library research marathon during which the student spent hours tracking down the available documents, filling out interlibrary loan requests, and reading in the rare books room. The concept of an assignment that could take an entire semester to complete is outside the realm of most students' understanding. The treasure-hunt approach to research and the satisfaction of finding the research treasure are long gone.

Students of today's universities, colleges, community colleges, and technical schools are rushed. Many have full- or part-time jobs; others have family obligations. Many of today's traditional students have been trained to expect instant results, if not instant gratification, when they want something. Today's students tend to be impatient. They have grown up in a world where fast is good and instant is better. The leisurely dinner is replaced by fast food. The delicious afternoon spent reading a novel is replaced by a ninety-minute made-for-television version of the book or the ever-present Cliff's Notes. The long, lazy drive to nowhere on a fall afternoon is replaced by a high-speed tour of the highways leading to the latest hot spot or cold spot for a quick look at the scenery. Students today want to get the information they need immediately by pushing a button.

Many of the resources students need to complete their higher-education assignments are now available in electronic format. They can be accessed via computer, and many times they can be accessed from outside the library building. This creates certain efficiencies for the students. They can save time by working from their dorm rooms, homes, or workplaces. They no longer have to visit the library to find information useful to their needs. They can work at their own pace and at times that suit their preferences and schedules.

Unfortunately for the future of research, not everything is available electronically. Some information is available only in paper, some information is available only on microform, and some information is available only in the library building. This creates a choice for the student. Most students understand that nonelectronic resources exist. But to use them, one must overcome the inertia involved in leaving home. This could be as simple as a one-minute walk to the library. However, many students today do not live in dorms or even in the same city as the university. In today's commuter and distance-education environment, travel to library resources can be a significant investment of time and energy. It may involve the complexities of getting a babysitter, catching a bus, finding a parking place, or taking time out of a normal schedule to get to the library during hours when it is open. The alternative is to stay home and limit oneself to what is available electronically.

By limiting themselves to the information that is available electronically, students limit the thoroughness of their research. It is not yet possible to exhaustively survey the literature of any discipline or topic by using electronic tools alone. Most students understand this, but many do not or cannot overcome the obstacles involved in traveling to the resources they could use in the library.

In an effort to obtain what is needed from home, many students will simply surf the Internet for information and accept anything they find, regardless of its quality. Of course, they will usually find information in abundance, but the quality of what they find will inevitably be mixed. Even though time seems to be of the essence for students, they would rather use copious amounts of time sifting through websites for something usable than make a trip to the library. The faster they can accomplish their assignments, the happier they are, even when the resulting products—and grades—are less than stellar.

Many students don't know how the library materials available electronically are different from those they find surfing the Web. Some students have never learned to use a periodical database or an online catalog. Unless they are taught the hows and whys of electronic resources, they are likely to use random websites for their information needs, thinking that one source is as good as another.

In the face of this situation, it becomes imperative for academicians to step in and teach students (1) how to find quality information using electronic sources and (2) that tools and resources exist in nonelectronic format. Using those resources may save them time and effort in the long run. Students need to see that the tool that seems to be saving them time may do so at the cost of achieving a good grade, because they have inexpertly selected the wrong tool for the job.

Evaluation of resources is critical to students' success or failure. Until this is understood, a student can succeed only accidentally. The benefit of using library-selected and -provided sources lies in the fact that those materials have been written by expert and reliable sources and chosen by expert and reliable professionals. The major evaluation considerations for library materials have already been accomplished by the time the student uses them. This evaluation process is invisible to students for the most part. This, coupled with the fact that so much information is available via the Web, makes students forget—if they ever knew—that not all sources are equally reliable or accurate. For that reason, librarians, instructors, and teaching assistants must be ready to explain this critical difference while training students in the more manual skills of pushing buttons and opening new screens.

It is for these reasons that this workbook has been written. We hope to assist others who are instructing students in the use of the new library tools as well as those who are teaching research methods and concepts. We offer exercises and explanations throughout the book to provide instructors with food for thought as well as ready-to-use or -modify exercises and examples. The exercises can be presented to an individual, a class, or a group of faculty members. They can be used as one-shot teaching opportunities or tied together in the context of a semester-long course. Those using the book for a semester-long course can shape some of the earlier exercises to be background for exercise

50, the Paper Trail Project, a culmination of the student's information literacy training. Each exercise has been used in the context of our own bibliographic-instruction sessions and, more frequently, in our three-credit semester-long course in information literacy. This book's appendix contains the Association of College and Research Libraries (ACRL) "Information Literacy Competency Standards for Higher Education, Standards, Performance Indicators, and Outcomes." Each exercise is based upon these standards, and the particular standards referenced are noted prior to each exercise.

We hope the content of this book will prove useful and beneficial and provide food for thought as we help mold students of all kinds into information-literate learners for life.

Chapter One
Information Explosion

Out in the vast world and beyond, there is an endless amount of information. We have the means to access more information than we will ever be able to process. Today, anyone can provide information to others anywhere in the world, on any subject, via the Internet. As the mountain of information gets larger and larger, people begin to suffer from what Richard Saul Wurman calls "information anxiety."[1] As with many other types of anxiety, having some knowledge and training—in this case, about information and its uses—can help reduce anxiety.

Transmission of information is not strictly a human trait. Many animals, birds, and even insects convey information to one another. Much of this information is very basic: "Go two clicks north to find good nectar." "You are in my territory—get out." "Look out, here comes a tiger!" These are basic survival messages.

In the earliest human groups, conveying these basic survival messages was all that was needed. People lived in small family groups widely scattered over the landscape. Contact with "outsiders" was probably infrequent for these mobile groups of hunters and gatherers. The number of messages necessary to share was small. The speed at which messages traveled was slow. Survival was the main concern.

When plants and animals were domesticated, people were required to stay in one place to care for them. They also had to stay in areas where water and food for the animals was available, so the number of places where people could settle was more limited. This resulted in larger gatherings of people in specific places. Locating in one geographic spot required more permanent structures to be built. Domestication of plants and animals also meant that it was possible to have a surplus of food to support the population. A sedentary lifestyle was less stressful for human reproductive systems. The human population grew as a result of all these changes.

As individuals or groups began to "own" things, the need for conveyance of information grew, as did the need for recording it. People needed new messages about geographic boundaries, water rights, whose animals were whose, and how to find the house of a relative or the next settlement. It became easier to "spread" information, and information spread faster because people were closer together. As populations grew, some people began to produce goods as well as food and clothing. Specialists produced tools or other items that helped workers of all kinds do their jobs better, faster, more economically, or just made life easier in general. As more tools were invented, more people were needed to make the tools. Eventually, the demand for specialty goods became so large that the specialists devoted all of their time to producing them. They no longer had the time to produce everything necessary for their own survival. Specialists became dependent on other people for production of things in which they did not specialize. Tools and other specialty items were exchanged for subsistence items such as food and clothing. In some cases, specialty items were sold for money, and the money was used to purchase needed subsistence goods.

During this time of economic and social change, known as the Industrial Revolution, great numbers of people made the switch from farming to manufacturing. A large part of the population began to produce nonsubsistence items. Those products had to be traded or sold for food, shelter, and clothing. To sell the nonsubsistence products required advertising—billboards, catalogs, handbills, and traveling salesmen.

These fundamental changes in the world's economy meant that more record keeping and knowledge of how to use the records were needed. More people learned how to read because it was both possible and necessary, at least for the wealthiest segments of the population. Innovations such as the telegraph and the train sped up communication and made it possible over long distances. It became possible for manufacturers to locate offices in more than one place.

People began to specialize in dealing with the various kinds of documents, books, and other information that were being produced. They also specialized in the analysis and application of the information contained in the documents. The storage of information grew in importance as well. Some information was centrally located. Other information was stored at distributed locations. Information needed in multiple locations required reproduction of that information, either manual or mechanical.

Recently, another fundamental economic and social shift has taken place, moving significant segments of the world's working population into service occupations. Storing, managing, manipulating, and understanding information are now the primary activities of many of the jobs performed by educated workers, while food production has moved into the economic background. Information flows quickly via radio, television, phone, and the Internet. With the amount of available information reportedly doubling every seven or eight years, the amount of information we will encounter during our lifetimes is almost incomprehensible.[2] This explosion of information has led to a huge increase in the number of workers who manage, analyze, and interpret it. Many have referred to the time in which we now live as the information age.

Globalization of information and communication networks has had a major impact on society. It is now possible to create an international working group in real time. Collaborations of people in countries around the world are a regular occurrence. Information, ideas, plans, and projects benefit from this ability to share and to offer views from many different perspectives. Sharing in real time allows new ideas and achievements to become reality in shorter and shorter periods of time. Major global problems can be addressed and solved and decisions can be made without any lag time. Students need training in collaborative projects as part of their information literacy training. They will almost certainly be called upon to work in groups in their jobs. Giving them some practice in group dynamics, cooperation, leadership, and problem solving and brainstorming will be of benefit to them in their lives after graduation. Information literacy will be a desirable quality for employers now and in the future.

DISCUSSION OF THE MANY AGES OF INFORMATION

Today, humans have gone far beyond the basic survival messages of earlier days. Humans have become information rich, at least in terms of volume. It is useful to set the stage for students by discussing these different "ages of information."

Goal: Students will learn the history of information and come to understand why it is important to them. Students will learn to ask questions such as, What can be done with this mountain of information?

Description: The questions listed in exercise 1 will focus students on the continuum of information. It will give them a sense of how humans arrived at the current stage of information overload and why it makes people anxious. Asking the same questions for each "age" will allow students to compare and contrast the different ages and stages of information.

Tips for conducting the exercise: This discussion should take place in class, using what the students already know about human groups and the kinds of information available during each time period. Creating a picture on a chalkboard or a flip chart may be useful. Draw small circles far apart to represent human groups and their information needs during the Stone Age, for example. Add in water, food, and shelter symbols as students suggest them. The pictures for each successive age should become more and more crowded.

This exercise addresses ACRL Standard 1, Performance Indicator 2.

TEACHING METHODS AND APPLICATIONS

Along with the changes in how information is produced and how people access it and put it to use, teaching practice has also changed. College-level instruction of the past was almost exclusively delivered by lecture. Students attended those lectures, took notes, did outside reading, and applied what they had learned in a term paper or final exam. This type of teaching has its usefulness, but recent studies have shown that students of all ages benefit from other types of instruction as well. Human beings learn using all five senses. When more than one sense can be engaged, it appears that learning, especially long-term retention of learning, improves. When translating this idea to the classroom, instructors have added new teaching methods to their portfolios. Rather than using lectures as an exclusive method of teaching, ideas like problem-based learning and active learning generate more student involvement in the learning process and result in better retention of material and better application of the concepts learned.

Problem-Based Learning

Problem-based learning involves giving students an assignment that allows them to explore a problem and solve it. The problem to be solved should require the use of information found in class lecture/discussion, reading, and experimentation. Assignments of this kind must be carefully crafted to ensure that the desired outcomes are achieved. Time is also a factor. This teaching method can be "scaled" to fit an entire semester, a few weeks, or a single class period. With a long-term assignment, the problem to be addressed can be larger. The methods used to solve the problem can be more complex. However, if the time available for the exercise is short, as it is with a single fifty-minute class period, the instructor must be very narrowly focused. Nevertheless, if the instructor sets specific time limits for each part of the problem-based learning process

and adheres to those limits, this type of exercise can be very useful.

Goal: For exercise 2 students begin with a problem that must be solved in a limited period of time. They must gather information, evaluate it for accuracy and reliability, and select the most appropriate sources to address the problem.

Description: Students will be given a situation that they might encounter in a work environment. They will be asked to gather information about a specific problem, using the Internet and other electronic resources available to them in the classroom. They will

---

Exercise 1

The Many Ages of Information

Stone Age	Agricultural Age
Industrial Age	Information Age

Compare the following considerations for each age:

1. What were the means of communication during this time?
2. What was the speed of the communication? What were the means for "spreading the word"?
3. What was the size of the audience?
4. How much information was transmitted in any one communication? (How big was the file?)
5. What was the purpose of transmitting the information?
6. How important was the need for an accurate and reliable answer?

---

have a limited time to gather information and evaluate it for appropriateness, accuracy, currency, reliability, and so on. They will select the "best" information. Their choice of information will be presented to the class along with their reasons for its choice. The class will discuss the sources and their quality and how this applies to information literacy. Each student or group will create a bibliography of the sources they chose, presented in a standard bibliographic format.

Tips for conducting the exercise: Divide the class into groups of three or four students. Set time limits for each section of the exercise (research, evaluation, bibliography creation, class presentation) based on the amount of time available. This exercise can be accomplished in a fifty-minute class session, but the instructor must be active in enforcing time limits. This exercise works best if the instructor specifies sources students may use: selected journal databases and specific websites, for example.

This exercise addresses ACRL Standard 2, Standard 3, and Standard 4.

Active Learning

Students retain information longer if they have more than one way of remembering it. Hearing something in a class lecture is one way of receiving information. Reading something in a textbook is another. Doing something oneself—finding answers, practicing skills, applying knowledge to complete a project—is another way to remember information. If instructors use a combination of these methods of presenting information, students retain and remember what they have learned better. After students hear about how a database works, for example, it is useful for them to have a relevant assignment that requires them to use the database. Active learning refers to having students actively participate in the learning process. It does not necessarily require physical movement outside of the classroom. It does require engaging the students' interest, getting their involvement in the process, and allowing them to express their questions, ideas, and opinions. Remember your grade-school field trips? They provided a new venue, a physical departure from the classroom, learning by observing, touching, smelling, tasting, and hearing in various combinations. This was active learning. It has translated to many college classrooms, to the benefit of students and instructors alike.

In active learning exercises, it can be useful to occasionally set students to an impossible task—a task that cannot easily be accomplished within the parameters set for the assignment. When they fail to accomplish the task, it causes them to wonder why they were asked to do it. This makes classroom discussion of the task much more relevant and interesting to them.

Free-range searching (see exercise 26, chapter 6—"Books and Catalogs") is an example of active learning that includes a combination of physical movement and problem solving. It awakens the competitive spirit in some students and usually causes an emotional response back in the classroom.

In general, making information literacy instruction student-centered, rather than instructor-centered, improves learning and retention for the students and makes the class more interesting and less predictable for the instructor.

Exercise 2

Finding the Best Information: Your Job May Depend on It

Imagine you are working in the office of the president of the university. You and several other workers act as the research team for the president. The president has been asked to take a stand on the issue of drinking on campus—to allow drinking on campus or not—and to present her decision to the board of governors at the monthly meeting at 5 p.m. tomorrow. She wants to know the relevant issues that surround the issue (health and safety, student rights, statistics, what other schools do, effect on student enrollment, and so on).

This is a critical issue, and your job may depend on how well you do with this assignment. You and your team must find three high-quality (accurate, reliable, timely) articles and/or websites that will help her make her decision and present them to her before she leaves the office today. You must be able to defend the information sources you select and say why they offer the best information on the topic. You must be able to speak to the quality of the information based on the author, the publisher, the sources cited, the timeliness, and the accuracy and reliability of the content.

You will also create a bibliography of the three sources you chose and cite them in MLA format, to be handed to the president with your presentation.

Adapted from an exercise created by Barbara F. Kenney, information literacy librarian, Roger Williams University, Bristol, Rhode Island.

TECHNOLOGY IN THE CLASSROOM

Contributed by Amanda K. Izenstark

Librarians charged with teaching information literacy may find themselves in one of several positions: meeting a particular class one time only, meeting a class several times, teaching a multisession course in person, teaching a course entirely online, teaching a "hybrid" course (a course that uses a mix of face-to-face and online teaching), or becoming "embedded" in (contributing to) a course that is online. Integrating technology appropriate to the course and students' needs can facilitate learning.

Technological change is inevitable, however, as the tools needed to support computing become smaller, more portable, and more available. Power that existed only in a desktop format a few years ago is now available in formats smaller (and lighter) than a textbook. In the not-so-distant past, students writing papers needed to purchase word-processing software, but now documents, presentations, and more can be created, edited, cited, and submitted using free web-based technology.

Web 2.0 has been both hailed and decried as user-centered and user-cluttered, but those same features that make Web 2.0 features so easy to use and interact with make them simple to adopt as learning tools. As with any program, activity, or technology, consider the goals and outcomes of the learning situation, and assess the use of the tools.

It is often assumed that students have used all of the technologies available and are already familiar with them by the time we see them in class. In reality, students of any age have varying levels of comfort with new technologies. Many are baffled when an interface changes and familiar functions have moved to unfamiliar places. When considering tools to use in the classroom—be it real or virtual—consider students' comfort levels and experience. Begin by selecting tools that have their own understandable help features, but also investigate video and tutorial sharing sites where experienced users may post tutorials that can help orient new users to unfamiliar tools.

The future holds even more tools and opportunities that can be harnessed and used to teach information literacy. It's worth remembering that what's current today may not be what's current tomorrow, so experiment and find what works for you.

Managing Courses

Some librarians may find themselves in a position to contribute to a class in an ongoing way, through repeated in-person or virtual visits. This may lead to becoming "embedded" in some fashion in a learning management system.

Learning management systems (LMS) have become a way to provide entire courses but also supplemental materials in classes, and many of the mainstream systems—such as Blackboard, Sakai, ANGEL, Desire-2Learn, and Moodle—offer tools that can be used to support information literacy instruction. Librarians may find themselves logged in to these systems with "permission" settings that allow complete access to information in these systems, or they may find themselves in more limited roles, such as that of a teaching assistant or a student. No matter what the role, the librarian should be aware of some basic commonalities.

Common tools include assignments and quizzes, while others offer portfolio tools that allow students to view and comment on other students' portfolios. Depending on the permissions allowed, a librarian may be able to create or collaborate on assignment creation or may be asked to develop a series of quizzes or surveys. If the role is the very limited student role, options still open to the librarian include creating and posting content and participating in chat sessions.

A librarian developing his or her own course will have much more flexibility, but if access to a class is granted, don't automatically assume that being given "student" status is an insult; privacy policies may have a role in the access a librarian may have to a class.

Regardless of the system, almost all offer some way of transferring exercises, assessments, and other content from one course or section to another, making it easier to reuse materials. Once an assignment or quiz has been designed, for example, the question sets can be downloaded and subsequently uploaded into other courses on the same server. This makes it simple to create one tool that can be used across multiple classes.

Interactive Technology in the Classroom

Classroom Management Software

Classroom management software (CMS), such as SynchronEyes, NetSupport School, LanSchool, and others, offer features that enhance classroom learning, including the ability to create groups of students for collaborative work and quick polls. Depending on the features of the software, students may be able to share files with others in their groups and deliver demonstrations to the class from their seats. These tools may also allow instructors to direct students to a particular resource simultaneously or administer a quiz and collect assignment submissions.

Features vary across programs. Many of these packages are tied to a specific installation in a specific classroom, but others allow connections outside of the classroom.

Collaboration Hardware and Software

Tools such as ClassSpot and TeamSpot allow users to collaborate on projects and view each others' screens, but they are not intended to have all of the classroom control functionality of CMS. Instead, they are created to encourage sharing and back-and-forth dialogue (albeit electronic). For collaboration tools that can be used in class and continue to be used outside of class, see below, "Encouraging Collaboration Digitally: In Class or Out."

Classroom-Response Systems, or "Clickers"

Clickers are devices used to gather instant responses to questions in a classroom. Used in a timely and appropriate manner, clickers can be useful to glean information from large classes, where not all students may have the chance—or be willing—to contribute. In smaller classrooms, where students may feel less intimidated about speaking up and discussion may occur freely, clickers may seem to be an unnatural interruption in the flow of the class.

If clickers are used, good question design and appropriate follow-up are essential. Clickers are generally best for yes/no, true/false, or multiple-choice questions, although some include calculation capabilities. Once answers have been displayed, further elaboration may be needed, especially if results are unexpected.

Interactive Whiteboards

In many classrooms, the use of the interactive whiteboard is the domain of the instructor, but with some guidance, these boards can help engage students and assist in the development of presentation and public-speaking skills. As of this writing, the novelty of these tools is still enough to get the attention of students, especially when used in conjunction with classroom control software that allows the broadcast of the projected image to students' computers.

Beyond the novelty factor is the ability for the presenter to get out from behind the lectern. Students (and some instructors) are inclined to use the lectern as a crutch, but the touch-screen functionality of interactive whiteboards encourages students to emerge from the corner to highlight and click on links, creating a more dynamic presentation. With the addition of electronic markers, students can "write" on the boards to emphasize points. To simplify the use of these boards while inside a web browser, type *about:blank* into the address bar of the browser to display a blank page. This page can be bookmarked for later access.

PDAs and Other Handheld Devices

Because handheld devices such as PDAs can store texts as well as perform planning functions, some medical and nursing programs have begun requiring students to own them. Some of these devices may be configured to work as classroom-response systems, allowing on-the-fly assessment. Because of the variability in systems, however, designing instruction that would include the use of PDAs or handheld devices may be limited to those campuses where each student is required to have a specific device and configuration.

Encouraging Collaboration Digitally: In Class or Out

Tools that allow users to collaborate electronically are a boon to teaching and learning, both in face-to-face classes and in distance education. Rather than requiring students to e-mail various versions of projects to other group members, these tools support simultaneous or asynchronous creation and editing, so each group member has access to the most recent version at any time. If the collaboration tools of a formal LMS aren't available, or you want to use an option that will allow students to access their information regardless of their institutional affiliation, free collaboration tools are available for a variety of tasks.

The key to selecting the right tool is to envision the eventual use. Is the focus on sharing the results of group survey research? Look to a collaborative spreadsheet tool. Is the goal a document that can be shared and updated as information changes, during the course and after? A wiki may be appropriate.

Keep in mind that privacy may be a concern when using these tools. If students register to use some of these tools under their real names, these may provide an opportunity for students to create a positive digital identity along with writing samples, but they may also invite unwelcome attention. Consider and discuss these issues before requiring students to use these technologies, or select tools that do not require registration.

Another consideration is the operating system students may be using. Generally, web-based tools that work in a browser have the fewest compatibility issues. Tools that need to be downloaded and installed are more likely to be subject to a user's computer configuration.

Please note that specific tools may change, so selection and examination of current tools may be needed to determine the best fit for a particular learning environment.

Collaborating on Documents, Presentations, and Spreadsheets

Collaborative document tools can be used for group papers, fact sheets, and other group projects. Students can create presentations with and for classmates in the same room or across the world. Once a final version has been created, the results can be printed, exported, "published" as a web page, or—in the case of presentations—embedded in other sites, using the links provided.

At the time of this writing, two products dominate this market: the Google Docs suite (http://docs.google.com) and the Zoho suite (www.zoho.com). With a Google account, users can create basic word-processing documents and presentations and invite other users to edit or collaborate with them. Zoho is less well known, but it offers much more functionality than the Google suite. Zoho Writer, for example, looks more like a full-featured word processor than Google Docs does, including various viewing settings that will look familiar to users of desktop software. Documents can be exported in a wide variety of formats, including LaTeX, which is used extensively in the scientific, technical, and medical (STM) fields. With functionality comes a steeper learning curve, however. Consider the skill level and needs of the audience when determining which tool to use.

Showing Data: Chart Tools

Basic spreadsheet software allows users to create and manipulate charts, but collaborative spreadsheet programs give students the opportunity to update and manipulate data at a time that's convenient for them. Google Docs includes collaborative spreadsheet and chart creation functionality, as does Zoho.

For broader chart creation options *without* spreadsheet functionality (which might be too advanced for some users), the website Chartle.net (www.chartle.net) allows individual users to create and share a variety of charts and diagrams, including Venn diagrams, which are helpful for visualizing search strategies. (The site is in beta as of this writing.)

Getting Students to Brainstorm and Illustrating Relationships: Mind- and Concept-Mapping Tools

Mind-mapping and concept-mapping tools can help students of all levels visualize relationships between ideas and concepts, or, at the very basic level, allow them to record ideas about a topic that they might have as they progress during their research. Some tools allow users to easily download their creations, or provide links to embed images in websites, blogs, or documents. Many institutions have licenses for the popular software Inspiration, but there are free alternatives.

Functionality varies between tools, with some offering collaborative features, such as the web-based bubbl.us (http://bubbl.us) and XMind (www.xmind.net). Others are meant for individual use, such as FreeMind (http://freemind.sourceforge.net).

Sharing Web Resources and Creating Webliographies: Social Bookmarking Tools

An easy way to create a course or group webliography is to use a social bookmarking site. Delicious (http://delicious.com) and other tools allow users to store their bookmarks remotely and create custom tags (or labels) for their bookmarks. Instructors can use tags to create a list of resources for a class, or they can suggest that students use a specific predetermined tag to categorize links in a way that will be accessible to other users of that tag.

Users of Diigo (www.diigo.com) can bookmark pages, but they can also annotate pages on other websites and then share those notes with others. Faviki (www.faviki.com) is a relative newcomer to the social bookmarking arena, but it has added semantic tagging functionality, allowing greater search and suggestion functionality to its users and enhancing serendipitous discovery.

Developing a Dynamic Document: Wikis

The most famous wiki is Wikipedia (http://en.wikipedia.org), beloved and notorious for its contents, which sometimes seem to shift on a daily basis. Wikipedia's underlying foundation is an open-source program, MediaWiki, which many individuals and institutions have installed on their own servers for their own purposes. In some cases, MediaWiki has been used to create competitors to Wikipedia, such as Scholarpedia (www.scholarpedia.org), Citizendium (http://en.citizendium.org), and Conservapedia (http://conservapedia.com). MediaWiki is one of several options available at the time of this writing.

If installing wiki software on a server isn't an option, there are other routes. Some learning management systems incorporate wiki functionality into their systems, making it easy for individuals or groups to create easily revised content that can be shared with the class but not shared with those outside the system. For example, groups investigating a topic can share and revise information as students uncover more research and resources.

For individual or small-group work outside of an LMS, PBworks (http://pbworks.com; formerly PBWiki) offers basic wiki functionality for free, with competitively priced educational plans.

Documenting Reactions and Facilitating Discussion: Blogs

Although many students have read blogs, others may not be aware that they've read them. Blogs can be used as a way for students to create individual or group research logs they can share with their instructor or with fellow students. If the instructor or librarian working with the class wants to monitor the blogs with minimal effort, a feed reader can be used to aggregate the RSS feeds from students' blogs, alerting the instructor when there's a new post.

Tools such as Blogger (www.blogger.com) and WordPress.com (http://wordpress.com) are freely available, but some institutions have installed blogging software on local servers. WordPress also offers local installation and configuration (http://wordpress.org), which allows more customization.

Creating and Delivering Small-Scale Surveys

A final way to engage students is to incorporate surveys and polls. Before covering a topic, polls and surveys can be used to determine class members' preclass knowledge, their experience with a topic, or their opinions toward an issue; or for student groups to survey other students in the class. This is particularly useful in distance learning, where using a classroom-response system would not be feasible. Although instructors can develop and push their own questions to the class, students could use surveys to determine how to target group presentations that would be delivered at a later date.

Tools available include SurveyMonkey (http://surveymonkey.com), which has a free basic subscription suitable for class use and annual subscription pricing for larger projects. Responses can be exported or displayed as charts. Google Forms (available through the Google Docs page, at http://docs.google.com) allows users to create forms for other students to fill out. The responses are deposited into a spreadsheet, which can then be used to create charts and display data.

Notes

1. Richard Saul Wurman, *Information Anxiety: What to Do When Information Doesn't Tell You What You Need to Know* (New York: Bantam, 1990).

2. Wurman, *Information Anxiety*, 32.

Chapter Two

What Is Information?

Information is everywhere. It is all around us. There are many mechanisms for conveying information and many reasons for wanting and needing it. But what is it?

This seems like a pretty simple question, but defining the term is not an easy matter. In discussions with students we have found that many have a rough idea of what they think information is, but very few are able to put their definition into words. Several approaches can be used to get students to think about the concept.

Goal: Exercise 3 requires students to consider the word *information* and its meanings. It will supply students with the "big picture" and make them understand that everything is information. The exercise should also get students to ask some questions about how to pluck specific straws of information out of the huge haystack of information that exists.

Description: Through group discussion, this exercise gets students talking and thinking about the nature of information.

Tips for conducting the exercise: The six parts of exercise 3 offer different approaches to the same concept. It is not necessary to have students complete more than one or two at most. For number 1, distribute index cards and give the instructions verbally. For number 2, distribute a list of nouns. Ask each student to select a word and decide whether it is or is not information. Have the class argue for or against the designation given. For number 3, break the class into small groups. Present each group with a set of objects and have them list the information each object might supply. We have included items on our lists that give students pause—dust, a diamond ring, a baby's footprint. Many students indicate at first glance that these are not information. When pressed to think about it, however, students can usually make a list of information that something as simple as dust might convey. Dust might inform you of long absence from a house, sloppy housekeeping, lack of allergies, environmental fallout, neglect, not a priority, lack of time, lack of money to hire a housecleaner, and more. The conclusion to be reached in this discussion is that everything is information. In number 4, divide the class into small groups. Ask students to list twenty things they think are information. Have group 1 list their "Top Ten" on the chalkboard. Have group 2 add anything new on their list to the list on the board. Continue through the groups until the list is exhaustive. In number 5, ask students, in groups or individually, to come up with a one-sentence definition of *information*. Have them read their definitions to the class. Then ask the class to merge all aspects of each definition into one comprehensive definition. In number 6, have students find a partner. Each pair of students will select an item from whatever collection of things the instructor cares to assemble. Ask students to use the worksheet to make lists of information that can be gleaned from the item, both actual and inferred.

This exercise addresses ACRL Standard 1, Performance Indicator 2.

INFORMATION ANXIETY

Information anxiety is that helpless feeling that comes with the realization that there is more information than one person can ever hope to process. "So much information, so little time."

Consider these estimates:

- More new information has been produced in the last thirty years than in the previous five thousand.[1]
- Close to a million books are published internationally each year.[2]
- In 2008 Google's link counter found one trillion unique URLs on the Web at one time.[3]

Do You Know What Information Is?

1. Name anything that is not information and write down your ideas on this index card. Each student will pass his or her card to the student on the right. The student receiving the card will tell the class whether he or she agrees with the assessment.
2. Select one item from this list of words. Explain why the item is or is not information.

parking ticket	baby's footprint	calendar
skeleton	college catalog	transcripts
ring	greeting card	floppy disk
dust	term paper	motorcycle

3. You have been given an object or a group of objects. Please make a list of information that the object(s) you have been given might supply.
4. Make a list of twenty things you consider to be information. Group 1 will record its "Top Ten" on the chalkboard. Each of the other groups will fill in or add to the list until it is exhaustive.
5. Please write a one-sentence definition of *information*. We will merge all statements into one that the class can agree on as a universal statement.
6. Take the role of a forensic scientist or archaeologist. (The job of a forensic scientist or archaeologist involves collecting physical evidence and applying a variety of known and sometimes unknown variables to the evidence to determine the importance of the evidence to an event.) Choose one item from the collection provided by the instructor. With a partner, list as many different pieces of information as you can get from the item. The information may be physically present, inferred, or implied. For example, use a piece of antique jewelry. List the following:

Physical characteristics—style

Creator or designer—known? unknown?

Age of the piece—vintage? antique? modern?

Gemstones—what kind? how many?

What other information is physically present, inferred, or implied? (For example, from a broken piece of antique jewelry, you can see that it is of a certain size, shape, and style. You should be able to name the kind of jewelry it is—a ring or a brooch. You might infer what kind of gem is in the piece, the age of the piece, and its value.)

Precious metals—platinum? gold? sterling?

Broken—what part of the piece is damaged? ripped or torn? smashed? broken with age?

Where was it found—trash? antique store or pawn broker? attic chest? vintage jewelry box or armoire?

- According to a recent article in the *New York Times*, "From the days of Sumerian clay tablets till now, humans have 'published' at least 32 million books, 750 million articles and essays, 25 million songs, 500 million images, 500,000 movies, 3 million videos, TV shows and short films and 100 billion public Web pages."[4]
- The amount of new information stored on paper, film, and magnetic and optical media almost doubled from 1999 to 2002.[5]
- A weekday edition of the *New York Times* contains more information than the average person was likely to come across in a lifetime in England in the 1600s.[6]
- In one year, the average American will read or complete 3,000 notices and forms, read 100 newspapers and 36 magazines, watch 1,572 hours of television, listen to 1,100 hours of radio, buy 20 CDs, talk on the telephone almost 192 hours, read 3 books, and spend countless hours exchanging information in conversations.[7]

The growth of written information is a historical phenomenon, not peculiar to modern times. What has changed is that we now have computerized information systems that can collect, manipulate, and generate information quickly and efficiently. We have broadcast media, computers, the Internet, satellite systems, and other technologies that provide extremely rapid access to information. These media literally surround us with information. The measure of the amount of information is so complex and changes so quickly that any calculation is almost instantly out of date. More of us are required to find, evaluate, and apply information than ever before.

OVERCOMING INFORMATION ANXIETY

Information anxiety is a feeling of being overwhelmed that comes when confronting a large information task. This exercise is designed to show students the first steps they need to take to overcome the information-anxiety barrier that goes up when they receive a complex assignment.

Goal: The goal of exercise 4 is to allow students to express their information anxiety and to collectively acknowledge that this feeling is normal—they are not alone. The exercise also shows students that thinking about and identifying key elements of an information-gathering task make it less daunting.

Description: Part 1 of this exercise confronts students with a huge research and writing assignment, which they are meant to think they have to complete. This will cause the onset of information anxiety. Part 2 of the exercise asks students to analyze how they felt when they received this assignment and to write those feelings down. Part 3 asks students to consider how to break this large assignment into small, prioritized elements that can be accomplished without anxiety.

Tips for conducting the exercise: Give your students part 1, ask them to read it over, and request questions after everyone has read it. Take questions for two minutes or less. Distribute the index cards for part 2. Allow students five minutes or so to read and accomplish the task. Then collect the index cards and read several of the responses aloud to the class. This usually lightens the students' mood, as some of the responses tend to be humorous, and students recognize that others felt the same sense of panic they did. The greatest relief comes, of course, when they learn that they are not required to do the assignment! Get the students to talk about why they felt as they did. Then distribute part 3 of the exercise. Ask students to write their answers individually for ten minutes at most. Discussion should follow, with students contributing ideas they have written. The instructor should emphasize the concept of breaking a large task into smaller pieces to make it less daunting.

This exercise addresses ACRL Standard 1, Performance Indicators 1, 2, and 4.

THE CHARACTERISTICS OF INFORMATION

Some information is factual. Factual information is a statement that can be proved. For example, the atomic weight of carbon is 12, and 2 + 2 = 4. Factual information will always be the same. It doesn't matter how many times you look it up or in how many different places. You will always find the same answer.

Some information is analytical. This information is an interpretation of factual information. For example, "Four out of five dentists surveyed recommended sugarless gum for their patients who chew gum." The facts are gathered and used together to arrive at some conclusion. Using analytical information takes some care and thought. If the U.S. Census Report says that families in the United States have an average of 2.7 children per family, what does that mean? Can there actually be .7 of a child? How many families were counted? How was the average found? Who did the calculation? It is important to consider what is actually being reported and how the analysts arrived at their conclusions. See figure 2.1.

Some information is subjective, meaning that it is presented from only one point of view. The informa-tion represents only one person's opinion or viewpoint. Your personal opinion that the best ice cream flavor is mint chocolate chip is subjective.

Objective information synthesizes information from a number of different sources and presents find-ings that can be replicated. For example, a researcher reports that she used five sources and that the authors in all five sources agreed on X. Another researcher could go back to those five sources and read about X in order to replicate the results presented by the first researcher. See figure 2.2.

WHERE DOES INFORMATION COME FROM?

Information often comes from direct observation or experience. This kind of information is known as *pri-mary*. The person having this information, or the diary, manuscript, or e-mail where it is first written down, is known as a *primary source*.

Information does not always come from a primary source. Many information sources collect, analyze, synthesize, and reproduce the information in a new form. The U.S. Census is a good example. Individu-als submit primary information about themselves and their families to the Census Bureau, which compiles the information in various categories. The Census Bureau does not report on each individual but rather reports the total numbers in each category. The infor-mation the Census Report provides is therefore *sec-ondary*.

Secondary information that is again collected, ana-lyzed, and repackaged is *tertiary* information. See fig-ure 2.3.

PRIMARY OR SECONDARY

It is important to know the number of times informa-tion has been synthesized or repackaged. Remember the children's game called "Telephone"? Children sit in a circle. The first child whispers a message into the ear of a second child. The second child whispers the message to the third child, and so on around the circle. The last child to receive the message says it out loud. The fun in this game is that the final message and the original message frequently have very little in com-mon. The more people the message passes through, the more garbled it is likely to become.

Exercise 4

Homelessness in Urban New England: Causes and Effects

Part 1: Write a Research Paper

In ten word-processed pages due in two weeks, explain the causes and effects of homelessness in urban areas of New England. Your paper must have a research question, thesis statement, introduction, body, and conclusion. Sources for your paper must be cited using MLA citation style and must include the following: five major books on the topic, five articles from appropriate scholarly journals, five high-quality websites, statistics, and five expert opin-ions on the topic. You must use the [name of institution] library to do this research.

Part 2: Write a Reaction

This task is daunting. You just got to campus! How can you possibly get this done in two weeks?

Please do the following: on an index card, write your reaction (your feelings) when you received this assign-ment. Do not write your name; your reactions will be anonymous.

Part 3: Break the Big Job into Smaller Tasks

1. List or circle in the text of the assignment any and all words or terms that a student would need to understand in order to accomplish this project.
2. List any and all things/tasks a student would need to know how to do in order to complete this assignment.
3. List any and all questions a student would need to have answered, expanded on, clarified, or otherwise restated in order to accomplish this task.

Unfortunately, this can also happen with more important information. When acquiring information, the researcher should be aware of the nature of the information, and if the information is not primary, the researcher should have some idea of how far it is from the primary source.

HOW INFORMATION IS PRESENTED: LET'S BUY A CAR!

Information can come in many different shapes and sizes. The same information can be packaged and shaped to suit the needs of the audience as well as the needs of the information provider. Just as a mother will tell her toddler "hot" instead of trying to discuss the thermodynamics of fire with him, so information providers package information to be appropriate to their goals and their audience.

Goal: Exercise 5 will illustrate to students the different ways information can be presented and how each one can be useful in appropriate circumstances.

Description: This exercise requires students to address a specific information need and to identify a source that will address that need.

Tips for conducting the exercise: Divide the class into small groups. Present students with the task of buying a car. Ask student groups to identify and write possible sources of information and where that information might be found, using the following chart. When students have completed their charts, ask groups to share their information needs and sources. Discuss the results.

This exercise addresses ACRL Standard 1, Performance Indicators 2 and 3, and Standard 3, Performance Indicators 2 and 4.

WHERE DOES THE INFORMATION COME FROM?

To continue the thought process from the previous exercise, students should be instructed to think about where the information comes from and who is responsible for it. Knowing how many times the information has been manipulated or what biases might be reflected in the presentation of the information is very important.

Goal: Exercise 6 will allow students to practice identifying different types of information from different sources.

Description: Give students a worksheet with the exercise on it. Ask them to write each item in the appropriate box, identifying each information item as primary, secondary, or tertiary and stating whether it is objective or subjective.

Tips for conducting the exercise: Note that the results from exercise 4 can also be used for this exercise.

This exercise addresses ACRL Standard 1, Performance Indicator 2.

INFORMATION QUALITY

How do students know when they have found information that answers their information need? How can

Exercise 5

Let's Buy a Car!

You've decided to purchase a used vehicle so you can get off campus. You know you don't have too much to spend—maybe a couple of thousand if you're lucky. What information do you need to make a purchasing decision?

1. In the first column, list all the information you would want or need to know about the car—things you won't be able to find out until you see it as well as things you might be able to research in advance.
2. In the second column, list different places you might find the answers to your questions (whom you might ask, where you might look it up, how you will find it out).

What You Want/Need to Know	Where and Who to Get the Information From

they select the best information from all the sources available? Students must examine the specific information need in order to answer these questions.

What Is the Information Need?

The sources of information and the specific information selected will be determined by the information need. Therefore, an information need must be clearly defined. Most students start with a general topic that gives a general frame of reference or a starting point. This general topic must be narrowed and clearly stated as a question based on the specific information needed. For example, a student may start with the topic "open-heart surgery." However, if the student really wants to

know about bypass heart surgery, then information about valve replacement heart surgery will not be relevant, even if the information is of high quality. If the student wants information about how many bypass operations were conducted in 2009, then information about the techniques used for making incisions in the human body is irrelevant. Making the topic specific and framing the search as a question can help identify the appropriate information. Using the specific question, the student will search for information that may answer that question.

What Information Is Appropriate?

Everything is information, but not all information is equally appropriate to use in every situation. So how does a student identify the most appropriate information? A student may find a book on the shelf, an article in a journal, or a website page. In thoroughly researching a question, a student may find an abundance of sources that will provide information. Sorting through the sources, evaluating those sources, and selecting the information that best supplies the answer to the information need are the heart of information literacy.

How Is Information Evaluated?

When information on a topic is identified and acquired, it is necessary to evaluate it. The evaluation process will tell the searcher whether the information is appropriate to answer the information need. The following questions need to be considered:

What Kind of Information Is It?

Information can be categorized to some extent. "Consider the source" is good advice. For example, some information is original or primary. Other information has been filtered, analyzed, processed, or selected by someone other than the original producer. This information is secondary. Information further removed from the original or information about information is tertiary. It must be stressed that the further removed the source is from the original, the more the information may have been changed.

Who Is the Author of the Information Found?

What credentials does this person have to answer your information need? Who is the expert on your topic?

Exercise 6

What Kind of Information Is It?

For each item on the list below, identify what kind of information it is and put it in the appropriate place in the grid.

diary
newspaper article
brochure about an
    appliance
advertisement in
    a magazine
scientific research article
recipe

billboard
college catalog
best-selling novel
book on the history
    of World War II
instructions left for
    the babysitter

	OBJECTIVE	SUBJECTIVE
Primary		
Secondary		
Tertiary		

Whose opinion do you want to rely on? Your mom might be the best person to ask how to feed a baby or how to create a budget, but is she the person to rely on for information about open-heart surgery? If she is a cardiac surgeon, she may be just the person. The point is, you must think about the author of the information and how likely it is that that person knows what he or she is talking about.

Who Is Supplying the Information for the Author?

Point of view is another concept to consider. When receiving information, you must note whether it is subjective or objective. At first, this may not be clear, and it may be other than it appears. Many times advertisers present a product as "the best," "the fastest," "the most reliable," and so on. The presentation of the advertiser can lead the unwary buyer to believe that the information has been presented objectively. However, the advertiser's job is to make the product seem like or sound like the best or the fastest or the most reliable. Advertisers get paid by the manufacturer of the product to do so. One can infer that their presentation of a product is somewhat biased.

In contrast, an agency whose job it is to compare a wide range of things, using equal criteria for each comparison and with no incentive from any manufacturer or seller, will present a more objective view of the products.

Why Is the Information Being Provided?

The next item to consider is why someone is providing information and who is supporting that person's ability to do so. For example, a doctor who works for the American Cancer Society and a doctor who works for the tobacco industry may provide very different information about the effects of smoking on the body. Both may have equally good credentials. Their reasons for providing the information may be very different.

Who Is the Audience for the Information?

Are you looking for something geared toward an audience of four-year-olds? The amount of information, the detail involved, and the language used will be different for an audience of four-year-olds than it will be for an audience of adults. Teen magazines may not appeal to members of the U.S. Supreme Court, because the Supreme Court is not the target audience for teen magazines. Again, language, subject, detail, and accuracy may all be influenced by the target audience.

Where Did the Information Come From?

Is the author the primary source of the information? Did the author use other sources in gathering information used in what he is telling you? If so, does the author tell you so and name the sources? If so, are the sources of information sources you would trust? Are

---

Figure 2.1

FACTUAL VERSUS ANALYTICAL INFORMATION

FACTUAL	ANALYTICAL
Consists of facts, and a fact is "the statement of a thing done or existing"	Interpretations and analyses of facts: interrelations among, implications of, and reasons for
Short	Usually produced by experts
Nonexplanatory	Often found in books and periodical articles
Often found in reference materials (e.g., encyclopedias) and in statistical information	

they also reliable and accurate? Is there a list of sources provided—a bibliography, for example—to which one can refer to check on details or obtain more information? Or do you just have to take the author's word for it that the information is correct?

In What Kind of Publication Is the Information Provided?

Is your information in a glossy magazine with lots of advertising? Is it in a clinical research journal supported by subscription or membership only? Is it from a website supported by a university or a special-interest group?

How Current Is the Information?

In some cases it doesn't matter how current the information is. If you are looking for the twenty-fifth decimal place in pi, it really doesn't matter when the calculation was done. The number should be the same in all cases if the calculation was done correctly. If you are looking for the temperature outdoors today, a temperature reading for last summer is not helpful. If you are performing open-heart surgery, having the most current information can be a matter of life and death. Knowing the currency of the information can help you put it in perspective. It can also help you decide whether it is appropriate to use it.

How Accurate Is the Information?

Again, in some cases, precision is not vital. If you need to know in general what time it is, almost any working clock will do. An Olympic speed skater, however, will obviously need an extremely accurate report on the time it took to complete her race. In gathering information, the greater the need for accuracy, the greater the number of sources that should be consulted. This is especially important if the researcher knows little about the subject. In most cases, to determine the accuracy of any information, at least two sources should be consulted.

THE QUALITY OF INFORMATION

The definition of quality information changes with the information need. Some information needs can be addressed only by an expert in a particular field. Some can be met by casual conversation at the water cooler with no expertise required. It is important to find information of the quality that suits the information need. The expert in a specific field may not be able to supply the appropriate quality of information for the discussion you have at the water cooler, and vice versa.

Goal: The goal of exercise 7 is to demonstrate the different degrees of quality in information and how each type of information might be useful in a given situation.

Description: Students will find that there are many sources that can provide information about their topic. However, some information may be more applicable than others under certain circumstances. This exercise will give students practice in finding sources of information appropriate to their information need.

Tips for conducting the exercise: Select several information topics for students to work on in pairs or small groups. Define an information need or question for each topic. Collect three sources of information on each topic and distribute them to the student groups. Sample topics might include the following:

Figure 2.2

SUBJECTIVE VERSUS OBJECTIVE INFORMATION

SUBJECTIVE	OBJECTIVE
Understood from one point of view	Understood from reviewing many different points of view

Is a 2008 Toyota Camry a reliable car? Supply one brochure from the Toyota dealer, one article from *Consumer Reports*, and one website from a Camry enthusiast.

Is using a credit card online dangerous? Supply one answer from a merchandiser (perhaps from its website), one article from a newspaper, and one article from a scholarly journal.

Is Microsoft really a monopoly? Supply one article from Microsoft, one article from a government perspective, and one opinion from a web chat room.

Discuss the findings on as many topics as you have time for. Collecting the information for a large number of topics can be very time consuming. Think about this exercise well in advance of its delivery date!

Exercise 7

Determine the Quality of Information

Please identify the information below about each of the sources given to you. If the information is not available and cannot be inferred, leave the space blank.

	SOURCE 1	SOURCE 2	SOURCE 3
Purpose			
Audience			
Authority			
Supplier			
Currency			
Accuracy			
Type of publication			
Primary or secondary			
Subjective or objective			
Quality of information (as relates to the information need). Does this source provide you with high-quality information?			
Usefulness of information (as relates to the information need). Does this source provide you with information that is useful in answering your queries?			

This exercise addresses ACRL Standard 1, Performance Indicator 2, and Standard 3, Performance Indicator 2.

Notes

1. Peter Large, *The Micro Revolution Revisited* (Totowa, NJ: Rowman and Allanheld, 1984).

2. University of California at Berkeley, School of Information Management and Systems, "How Much Information?" (Berkeley: Regents of the University of California, 2003), www2.sims.berkeley.edu/research/projects/how-much-info-2003/printable_report.pdf.

3. Jesse Alpert and Nissan Hajaj, "We Knew the Web Was Big . . . ," Official Google Blog, July 25, 2008, http://googleblog.blogspot.com/2008/07/we-knew-web-was-big.html.

4. Kevin Kelly, "Scan This Book!" *New York Times*, May 14, 2006, www.nytimes.com/2006/05/14/magazine/14publishing.html.

5. University of California at Berkeley, "How Much Information?"

6. Richard Saul Wurman, *Information Anxiety: What to Do When Information Doesn't Tell You What You Need to Know* (New York: Bantam, 1990), 32.

7. Linda Costigan Lederman, "Communication in the Workplace: The Impact of the Information Age and High Technology on Interpersonal Communication in Organizations," in Gary Gumpert and Robert S. Cathcart, eds., *Interpersonal Communication in a Media World*, 3rd ed. (New York: Oxford University Press, 1986).

Figure 2.3

CHARACTERISTICS OF INFORMATION

PRIMARY	SECONDARY	TERTIARY
Information in its original form when it first appears Has not been published anywhere else or put into a context, interpreted, filtered, condensed, or evaluated by anyone else Examples are a professor's lecture, newspaper articles written by people at the scene of an event, the first publication of a scientific study, an original artwork, a handwritten manuscript, letters between two people, someone's diary, or historical documents such as the U.S. Constitution.	Has been removed from its original source and repackaged Restates, rearranges, examines, or interprets information from one or more primary sources Examples are your classmate's notes on a professor's lecture, a newspaper article reporting on a scientific study published elsewhere, an article critiquing a new CD, an encyclopedia article on a topic, or a biography of a famous person. Also, secondary information leads you to primary information. Examples are an index to newspaper articles, an index to articles from scientific research journals, or a bibliography of an author's original works.	Even further removed from the original information than a secondary source Leads you to secondary information Examples are a bibliography of critical works about an author, an index to general periodical articles, or a library catalog.

Chapter Three
Getting Ready for Research

Planning is the key element to producing a good research paper, report, or presentation. However, planning is not a strong suit for many students. It takes time, it takes practice, and it seems irrelevant when faced with a formidable task such as writing a twenty-page term paper. The daunting task of producing that many pages of writing is overwhelming to most people.

The anxiety about taking on a big project is difficult to overcome. Many students have years of real-life experience. A growing number of students are older individuals responsible for a job, family, home, and car. People take on many difficult and complicated tasks every day. When confronted with a scholarly task, however, students frequently assume that the process is something new, something completely different from anything they have done before, and they become intimidated.

To make matters worse, students often wait too long to begin their research. Beginners often have no concept of how long the information-collection phase of their project is going to take. As normal humans, students put off tasks they see as difficult and unpleasant. So students may have to rush to find sources, take the first sources that appear, select quotes from those sources without regard to the context in which they were said, and insert them into their own text—where they may or may not support the argument the writer is trying to make.

RESEARCH PROCESS ANALOGIES

Many students have experience with research, though they don't know it. They have done complicated research to achieve an end goal (such as searching for colleges to attend), but it may have been for a truly nonacademic purpose. By using the "Research Analogies" exercise, you can help students make the connections between the nonacademic and academic research process.

Goal: Exercise 8 illustrates how the academic research process relates to similar processes in everyday life. It builds confidence and allows students to see the

Exercise 8

Research Analogies

Goal to Be Completed: (from the index card you received)

For example, "Open a new bank account."

Please list all of the "ingredients" that are necessary to complete the goal.

For example, (1) cash or checkbook, (2) personal identification, (3) bank's brochure listing types of accounts available, and so on, (4) bank location, (5) bank hours of operation.

1. _____
2. _____
3. _____
4. _____
5. _____
6. _____
7. _____
8. _____
9. _____
10. _____

Now list the steps necessary to complete the goal.

For example, (1) find a list of banks in the area, (2) pick the one that is most convenient or offers the best terms, (3) read the types of accounts the bank offers, (4) meet with a bank employee to open the account, (5) fill out the necessary forms, (6) write a check, and so on.

1. _____
2. _____
3. _____
4. _____
5. _____
6. _____
7. _____
8. _____
9. _____
10. _____

applicability of the scholarly research process to reality. It helps to overcome the anxiety and procrastination associated with "doing research."

Description: The following activity is meant to give students practice in recognizing everyday steps to successful research. Have students use an index card to list in detail the steps and actions they would take to fulfill the goal listed on the card.

Tips for conducting the exercise: The instructor should introduce the concept by briefly describing the panic with which a student receives the assignment of a major research paper and then following the uneducated path an imaginary student might take in getting the job done. This should be done with humor if possible. Errors should be exaggerated. Common fallacies should be emphasized. (Oh my, I can never do this—I'll wait until next week. Oh no, I only have a week to write this paper. What do you mean, the library is not open at 3 a.m.?) The exercise should then be introduced with special attention to the analogy aspect—if you can do one of these everyday tasks, you can do research. The instructor should do an example with the class before the teams try it themselves in order to illustrate the detail with which the steps need to be considered. An outline of the research process should follow the exercise so the common factors in the processes can be seen clearly. (Figure 3.1, following exercise 8, outlines the research process. Instructors can hand it out to students.)

After students have gathered the ingredients and listed the steps necessary to complete each task, have the groups report back to the class with their findings. They will soon notice that whether the task was "Put on Your Socks and Sneakers" or "Plan a Clambake for Twenty," each one has numerous ingredients and multiple steps. In life students accomplish a multitude of complex tasks every day. If they have the proper ingredients and know the steps to doing academic research, they will be successful in their research goals as well.

This exercise works best when done by pairs of students, but small groups work as well. Discussion should be encouraged. Although this assignment could be done outside of class, it helps to have the instructor on hand to guide the small groups, keep the work on task, and call time.

Here is a suggested list of "tasks to be completed":

- Change a baby's diaper.
- Make a quilt from scratch.
- Make a pan of lasagna.

- Plan a camping trip to Acadia National Park.
- Put on your socks and sneakers.
- Plan and give a fiftieth-anniversary party for your parents.

This exercise addresses ACRL Standard 1, Performance Indicator 1, and Standard 4, Performance Indicator 1.

Figure 3.1 is a handout for students when they are learning the research process.

ESSENTIAL QUESTIONS FOR RESEARCH

Students often have difficulty in framing a research question. They may have selected a topic, but it is difficult for them to narrow their focus from the general topic to a more specific question. Getting students to ask essential questions about what they need to know is a skill that will help them, no matter where they go or what they do. The following is an exercise to help them learn to ask those essential questions.

Goal: Exercise 9 teaches students to ask three essential questions when they begin the information-seeking process: What do I know? What do I need to know? How will I find out?

Description: Obtain five glass (or clear) jars with tight-fitting lids, such as Mason jars. Before class, fill each jar with water. To begin the exercise, arrange the class in five groups and give each group a jar. Ask each group to appoint a spokesperson and a recorder. Give each group a card with instructions not to open the jar but to observe the jar and to discuss the question "What is in the jar?" as best they can given what they think or know. After five minutes or so, give each group a second card that provides a point of view for them to think about the jar. Each group will receive a different point of view. Here are some examples to use:

Group 1: You are the soon-to-be owners of lots of land in a new development. You each plan to build your family homes on the land. The contents of the jar are taken from the stream that runs through the development.

Group 2: You are the owners of the development. You stand to make a considerable sale for each lot of land.

Group 3: You are the members of the Town Building Inspection and Zoning Board of Review that oversees the zoning of the new development. The development in question borders a major highway that is being rebuilt.

Group 4: You are administrators at the local state university. The development is important to you because you need more available housing for new faculty.

Group 5: You are the state's Department of Environmental Management. Your job is to enforce regulations that ensure that there is enough water and enough good water for the town.

As each group discusses the possible contents of the jar, the instructor should circulate among the groups and encourage students to provide the recorder with their ideas about what they think of the contents of the jar.

Ask each group spokesperson to report to the class by first introducing his or her group's assigned point of view and then telling the class what the group members think about their jar's contents. Lead a discussion of all the groups' ideas, and ask them to share what questions came up during their discussions. Ask a student to help you to record all the main ideas and questions on an easel pad or whiteboard (or by projecting a Word document on a screen). You will likely get many questions stemming from the students' lack of information and knowledge about the jars' contents. List these questions on the board. Ask students to review the list and decide what the major task for all groups should be. This should provide you with a perfect opportunity to turn these frustrations into the following questions: What do you need to know? How will you find out?

Conclude the exercise by asking students to identify the most important questions they need to ask to solve their group's information problem. You will need to assist them by asking leading questions: What do you know? What do you need to know? How will you find out?

Conclude the exercise with a wrap-up question: How can these three questions be used in future research projects?

Tips for conducting the exercise: Groups should have no more than three students each in order to facilitate engagement. This exercise takes approximately thirty minutes to accomplish: two five-minute periods are allotted for the groups to observe the containers and

Figure 3.1

THE SUCCESSFUL RESEARCH PROCESS

KEYS TO YOUR SUCCESS

Research is always a multistep process.

Research is often interdisciplinary.

Think broadly about your topic; then narrow and refine the focus.

Keep a record of everything you find and where and how you find it.

STEPS TO YOUR SUCCESS

Identify Your Topic

The topic is the idea that you are researching. Example: Pollution in the ocean.

Brainstorm and create a concept map of the topic.

Think about and visualize your topic from many different angles.

Note related and interrelated topics.

Note terminology and synonyms that can broaden your searching power.

State your topic as a question. Example: How does pollution affect the ocean?

Refine the question. Example: How does oil pollution affect marine life in the ocean?

Identify key concepts and list synonyms for them. Example: ocean, seawater; pollution, oil spills; marine life, organisms, biology, plants, animals, fish, mammals.

List disciplines or subject areas that relate to part of your research. Example: oceanography, environment and life sciences, fisheries, natural resources, marine affairs, biology, aquaculture, business.

Gather Background Information

Get a broad overview of the subject or topic.

Use both general and subject-specific encyclopedias and dictionaries.

Get more focused, in-depth, or historical background on the topic.

Use books written in the time period and follow up with more recent information.

Focus Your Research

Gather up-to-date, current information on the topic.

Use appropriate periodical information from popular, trade, and scholarly sources.

Use high-quality, appropriate web sites.

Gather in-depth, focused information on the topic.

Search for research studies, surveys, and experiments about your topic.

Evaluate Your Sources

Does the author have authority on the topic?

What are the author's credentials?

Is the information accurate for when it was written?

Is there a consensus of opinion on this topic? What are the important ideas?

What is the purpose of the source? How will it impact your research?

Is the purpose to inform, to entertain, to teach, or to influence?

Who is the author writing for? Is it biased in any way?

Has the author looked at the material objectively?

Does the author offer several points of view?

How does the source help answer your research question?

Does the source provide valuable, relevant information?

Does the source answer a part of the total research question?

make notes and judgments, and twenty minutes are allotted for groups to share information and to wrap up for discussion.

This exercise addresses ACRL Standard 1, Performance Indicators 1 and 4.

TOOLS FOR BACKGROUND INFORMATION

At the initial stages of research, general information is necessary, especially for the beginning researcher, who may have little or no knowledge of the topic. A typical example of a general-information tool is an encyclopedia. An encyclopedia article about abortion, for example, should provide enough description to suggest narrower categories of inquiry. It might also suggest the size and scope of the general topic. A subject-specific encyclopedia would give more precise information relevant to the discipline in which the topic falls. For example, a medical encyclopedia would emphasize the medical aspects of abortion, while a social-sciences encyclopedia would examine social aspects, and a psychological encyclopedia would deal with psychological aspects of the topic. Simply learning that discipline-specific encyclopedias and dictionaries exist is usually a revelation to students new to research.

USING ENCYCLOPEDIAS FOR BACKGROUND INFORMATION

The encyclopedia's main use is to provide an overview of a subject or topic. In addition, encyclopedias can introduce language specific to the research subject area. Knowing the language and terminology of their research area can aid students in designing their research question.

Goal: Exercise 10 will allow students to begin learning basic search skill strategies and to provide themselves with both background knowledge and terminology in the subject area.

Description: This exercise is an introduction to several basic skills such as keyword searching, using call numbers, and evaluating information. These skills are then used to find encyclopedias that will (1) provide background knowledge on the subject and (2) provide some relevant language and terminology that will help in further defining students' topic ideas.

Exercise 9

Developing Essential Questions for Information Seeking

In your group, have one person be the "recorder"—the person who will write down all your observations and conclusions. Have one person be the "reporter." This person will report your findings and conclusions to the class.

1. You have been given a jar containing a liquid. Without opening the jar, observe its contents and discuss what substance might be in it. Write down your ideas.
2. When you receive your "point-of-view" card, discuss what your thoughts are about the contents of the jar from this point of view. Record all ideas and suggestions.
3. When time is called, be prepared to report the findings from your group to the class.

Adapted from an exercise by Libby Miles, chair of the Writing and Rhetoric Program, University of Rhode Island, Kingston, Rhode Island.

Finding Encyclopedias for Background Information

Research Topic: _____

Purpose

- To gain background information, additional terminology, greater understanding, and context for your research topic using general and subject-specific encyclopedias
- To evaluate information sources for both relevance to your topic and quality of information
- To improve information-searching skills

Part I: Finding Relevant Encyclopedia Articles for Background Information

1. In the reference section of the library, find your research topic in the *New Encyclopaedia Britannica* or other general encyclopedia.
2. Using the keyword search method demonstrated in class, identify and locate a topic-relevant/subject-specific encyclopedia.
3. In each encyclopedia, find an article that meets your information need.
4. Read the articles and evaluate them within the context of your information need and according to the evaluation criteria discussed in class.
5. Photocopy the title page of both encyclopedia volumes.
6. Photocopy the first page of both articles.
7. Complete the table below.

	GENERAL ENCYCLOPEDIA	SUBJECT-SPECIFIC ENCYCLOPEDIA
Encyclopedia title		
Article title		
Author (if any)		
Volume in which article appears		
Year of publication		
Call number (on spine)		
List five words or phrases from the article that you believe are specific to your topic.		
Does the article offer any major ideas about your topic? List them here.		
Check for any additional authors and their credentials for further research. Photocopy if available.		
Note if the article includes any additional readings, bibliographies, suggested books, or websites. Photocopy if available.		
Which article is more useful? Less useful?		

Part II: Reporting the Results of the Encyclopedia Search

Using MLA citation format, cite the *more useful* article.

1. Summarize the encyclopedia article in a paragraph or two.
2. Write a one-page research-log entry that discusses both of the following:

   a. How you searched for and located both the encyclopedia and the actual article—discuss both your thinking and your actual searching. Was it straightforward? Any difficulties? Any questions?

   b. Your reasons/rationale behind your choice of the "more useful article." Evaluation criteria? Relevance to your topic? Extent of information?

Tips for conducting the exercise: Show students a variety of encyclopedias, beginning with general and moving on to subject-specific sets, covering two or three different subjects. Examples could include organized crime, civil rights, and nutrition. The subjects should illustrate the range of possibilities available. Use examples that you know are covered well in your collection of encyclopedias. Using a specific article, show students how to identify the author (if the article is signed), the coverage and scope, and the date of publication. Be sure to show students at least one online encyclopedia. If you show Wikipedia, be sure to discuss how it is different from other encyclopedias, where the information comes from, and the pluses and minuses of relying on this kind of information.

Demonstrate a simple keyword search in the library catalog for "encyclopedia AND crime" or "encyclopedia AND nutrition" to help students locate subject-specific encyclopedias relevant to their research topics.

From the bibliographic record in the online catalog, demonstrate how to identify what the library call number is for the encyclopedia and where the reference collection is in your library.

The creation of a clear and concise statement or question that will focus the research or project is another task that requires practice. Beginners may have difficulty in selecting the crucial ideas and key concepts in a general discussion or reading. Getting students to think about general topics and how they break down into smaller concepts is something that also needs to be taught. The ever-present freshman paper on "Abortion" is meaningless unless it is subdivided into manageable pieces. It takes several steps from "I think I will write my report on abortion" to a topic that will focus on a particular issue concerning abortion or a particular question to be answered.

This exercise addresses ACRL Standard 1, Performance Indicator 2; Standard 2, Performance Indicator 2; and Standard 3, Performance Indicator 1.

EVALUATING INFORMATION SOURCES

Contributed by Kate Cheromcha

Evaluation of information is essential from the beginning of any project. In research, each of the sources that students select must be evaluated for a variety of criteria: authorship, credibility, accuracy, reliability, currency, timeliness, scope, coverage, and relevance. It is useful to have students begin to think about evaluating the reliability and accuracy of every source of information.

Goal: In exercise 11, students will explore Wikipedia, how it is created, and what the advantages and disadvantages of this type of "community-built" encyclopedia might be.

Description: Many students use Wikipedia as their first go-to resource for research. This exercise enlightens students that all resources must be evaluated, some more than others! The Wikipedia exercise allows students to see both the strengths and weaknesses of this type of tool in research.

Tips for conducting the exercise: If students have not been assigned a research topic, suggest current issues that relate to the subject area they are studying. Often, current issues and/or controversial topics are useful for this exercise.

This exercise addresses ACRL Standard 3, Performance Indicators 2, 4, and 6.

Exercise 11

The Wikipedia Challenge

There is no dispute that Wikipedia contains a great deal of useful information. But how can you be certain of the credibility of that information? One way is to evaluate it. However, because of the nature of this information source, there are unique aspects that you must consider when evaluating it.

1. Search Wikipedia to locate any article that is relevant—even if just barely relevant—to your topic.
2. Read about Wikipedia in its own article, "Researching with Wikipedia," at http://en.wikipedia.org/wiki/Wikipedia:Researching_with_Wikipedia. In the section "Special research considerations concerning Wikipedia" read how to "Examine an article's history." Determine if anyone has made any changes or edits to your article.
3. Evaluate your Wikipedia article according to Wikipedia's recommended criteria (attached and also available at http://upload.wikimedia.org/wikipedia/en/1/16/How_to_evaluate_a_Wikipedia_article.pdf).
4. Read about the policy from the history department of Middlebury College, concerning using Wikipedia as an information source, from InsideHigherEd.com (Scott Jaschik, "A Stand Against Wikipedia," InsideHigherEd.com, January 26, 2007, http://insidehighered.com/news/2007/01/26/wiki). Be sure to skim through the posted responses!
5. In a short essay (100–150 words), answer the following questions: Does the Wikipedia article have any value or serve any purpose for your research? Why or why not? In answering these questions, consider the also following:

    Does this article meet Wikipedia's own evaluation criteria?

    Does this article have a history of changes and edits? Recently? Extensively? Can you determine who made the changes—and why? Check out how Microsoft tried paying a blogger to "correct" its Wikipedia entry as seen in this report from CBS news: www.cbsnews.com/stories/2007/01/24/tech/main2392719.shtml?source=RSSattr=HOME_2392719.

    Can you determine the author? The author's credentials?

    Does the article provide any references, additional readings, or sources?

    If there are links to other websites, what type of websites are they? Commercial? Educational? Other?

CONCEPT MAPPING

Students who are at the beginning stage of research are often overwhelmed with ideas that they are considering for topics. A concept map can help them organize their ideas and see the relationships between ideas.

Goal: Exercise 12 allows students to spend time formally engaged in brainstorming the broad research topic. Generating and identifying a variety of specific topic ideas from the broader subject push students to focus on a single idea or to combine several ideas to create a more interesting topic.

Description: Students will select a general topic. In the center of a large piece of paper, students will write their topic word or phrase. They will then write any and all words or phrases they can think of that relate to the central word or phrase. Using boxes, lines, and arrows, students will connect or group ideas that go together, relate to each other, or are subgroups. Students will then select the groups or combinations that have the most appeal for further research.

Tips for conducting the exercise: For this exercise, students may use a variety of marking tools. Pencils with good erasers, colored pencils, felt markers, or crayons work well. Some students have used sticky notes to jot down initial ideas and then moved the notes around to develop their maps. Each student will need a large sheet of newsprint paper. There are also computerized software packages that allow concept mapping (see chapter 1, "Getting Students to Brainstorm and Illustrating Relationships: Mind- and Concept-Mapping Tools"). Students should be instructed to write down at least four subtopics surrounding their main topic. Each of the four subtopics should have at least three to four subdivisions as well.

This exercise addresses ACRL Standard 1, Performance Indicator 1.

Figure 3.2 is an example of a concept map on the topic "Vegetarianism."

IDENTIFYING DISCIPLINES AND SUBJECT AREAS

Students are generally open-minded and willing to stretch their minds during the concept-mapping process. After the process, students should have a target topic, a small number of subtopics, and an interest in pursuing an area of inquiry.

Beginning researchers often skip steps that will actually save them time in the long run. One step that can help students prepare to write an effective research question is to consider the disciplines or subject areas that are likely to include their topic of choice. For example, if the topic is "Child Labor and the Silk Trade," all three disciplines of humanities, social sciences, and science are likely to consider some aspect of this topic.

Goal: In exercise 13 students will identify the academic disciplines and subject areas that will help them answer their to-be-developed research questions.

Description: Give students a handout with a description of the major disciplines and the subjects that fall into those disciplines. Using the catalog of your institution, have the class examine the various departments listed and place each department in a discipline. Then have students use a sample research topic to determine which departments on campus might produce information on that topic.

Tips for conducting the exercise: Have access to print and online formats of your institution's annual catalog of programs and courses. This exercise is best carried out as a discussion. Provide definitions of the disciplines from a dictionary such as *Merriam-Webster Online* (www.merriam-webster.com).

This exercise addresses ACRL Standard 1, Performance Indicator 2, and Standard 3, Performance Indicators 3 and 7.

FORMULATING A RESEARCH QUESTION USING CONTEXT

It is necessary to do some preliminary research simply to select a topic. Most students decide on their topic first and then try to find out if there has been anything written on that subject. They are loath to change or modify their topics, even when they find it impossible to locate materials they need. They are unwilling to use their time to do work that might prove to be of no use in the end. The instructor must show them how this initial legwork will improve the final product and save them time in the long run.

Students are equally unwilling to iterate a change in their topic when they find an overwhelming amount of information. Students may not understand that abortion in and of itself is a meaningless topic. Some work needs to be done to discover that medical and social issues surrounding abortion are two distinct areas of inquiry. The social issues further subdivide into many smaller segments. Until the student does this preliminary investigation, it is impossible to determine exactly what are the themes of the paper or the project to be completed. Definition of the topic proceeds from general to specific, but, again, some practice is necessary to make clear how increasing specificity will help in the acquisition of information pertinent to answering the need for information.

Goal: In exercise 14 students will learn to develop a research question that is open-ended and gives meaning to the topic they are researching.

Description: The exercise includes a series of questions that will lead students through the process of mentally and visually broadening, narrowing, and restricting the topic ideas that they began to develop during concept mapping. After this exercise, the worksheet in exercise 15 introduces the concept of Boolean searching and the idea that synonyms and closely related terms can help uncover more ideas on the topic.

Step 1: The instructor describes and illustrates a general topic that could be used for a research paper or project. Create a handout, PowerPoint presentation, or other tool to demonstrate the question development. It will be most effective if the examples are left out of the handout or PowerPoint, allowing the instructor to ask students to help fill in the examples.

Example: Discuss with students the topic of anabolic steroids in sports. This is a topic of popular interest to college students and can easily be used as an academic research topic. Students will need to transform the casual question "What do you think of those players who got named for using steroids?" into a question that allows them to tackle an issue, attempts to solve a problem, and provides the information they need to make a knowledgeable statement or response to the question. The question should follow a path: topic, subtopic, issue or problem, and finally question.

Figure 3.2

CONCEPT MAP

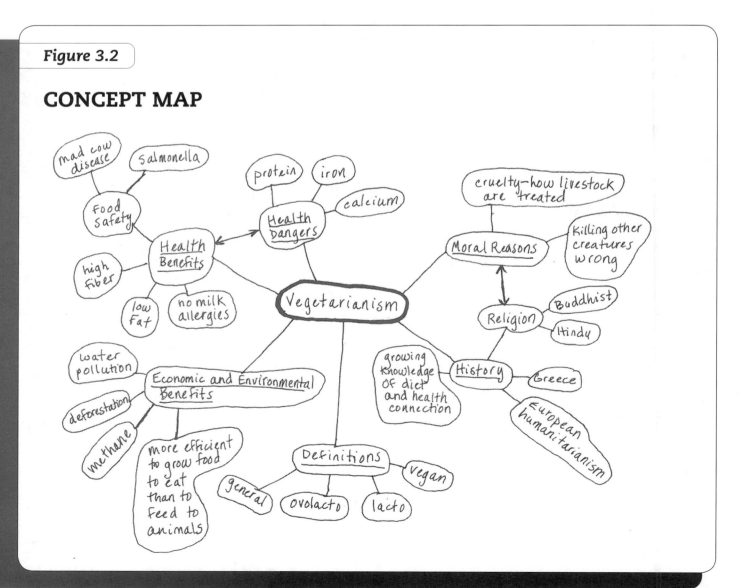

Refer to the chart in exercise 14 to see how to restrict and narrow a broad research topic. Once the general question has been established, consider how to clarify the issue or problem. Different types of questions can help refine and shape the direction of the research:

- Comparison questions (How does the long-term health of players who used steroids compare with those who did not?)
- Cause and effect questions (What affect have the steroid investigations had on baseball players' morale?)
- Measuring questions (To what extent has the steroid-use crisis impacted fans' expectations of the players?)
- Process questions (How are players monitored for steroid use and educated about the dangers of steroid abuse?)

Check to be sure that the research question meets these criteria:

- It is open-ended (cannot be answered with simple yes or no).
- It addresses an issue or controversy and/or solves a problem.
- It is something the student can take a stand on.

Tips for conducting the exercise: Other topic examples for illustration: No Child Left Behind and student achievement, dowry murder and Hindu culture, and city parks and economic benefits.

This exercise addresses ACRL Standard 1, Performance Indicator 1; Standard 3, Performance Indicator 3; and Standard 4, Performance Indicator 1.

Exercise 12

Create a Concept Map

Most people do not think in a linear style when they are working creatively. We think by linking groups of ideas together, "webbing" or "linking" a path to the final subject and topic idea. You will be joining all that you already know with what you learn during your research to build a more complete landscape of the topic you are working on.

Concept mapping helps you create a visual design, picture, or diagram of the thinking you are engaged in so you can reflect, sort, and refocus the ideas easily. Use this concept-mapping exercise to allow your brain to "free-think" along the way to the development of a research question.

Phase I: Brainstorming Instructions

In the center of the newsprint sheet, write down the most important word, short phrase, or symbol that relates to the subject idea you want to research. Draw a circle around this main idea.

Take a minute or two and think about what you put down on the paper. Thinking freely, without any expectation of the result, write or mark any and all related words, concepts, or symbols outside the circle. Write anything you can think of that is even remotely related to the topic idea. Come up with at least four subtopics that relate to your main idea. For each of your four subtopics, think of three to four subdivisions that fall under the subtopics.

Now draw squares around single ideas and circles around groups of ideas.

Use lines to connect these items to the main idea and to groups of related ideas.

Use arrows to interconnect ideas or to form subgroups of ideas.

Leave lots of white space so your concept map has room to grow and develop.

Don't worry about being exact or perfect—don't analyze the work!

Phase II: Editing or Refocusing

Think about the relationship of "outside-the-circle" items to the center item.

Erase and replace or shorten words to some key ideas.

Relocate important items closer to each other for better organization.

Link symbols with words to clarify relationships.

What are you thinking about now? How is your topic developing?

Now proceed to topic analysis to further develop your research question!

DISCOVERING SEARCH TERMS

Once a topic and question have been established, students frequently attempt to use their research question to search for information. As most search engines are keyword driven, the results of natural language searching are less than optimal. Students must learn

Exercise 13

Disciplines and Subject Areas

Now that you have started to gather some topic ideas for your research question, you need to consider where the answers are likely to be found. Before you can know what type of books, periodicals, and websites to use, you must consider a larger question. What disciplines or subject areas will help to answer the different aspects of your research question? Recognizing the three major disciplines (humanities, social sciences, and science) will help clarify how these areas of knowledge are defined and where your research topic fits in. It will help when you begin to gather information by making it easier to identify some broad-based sources such as encyclopedias.

Review your institution's catalog of academic programs and courses. All of these fields of knowledge fall into one of the three major disciplines listed above. Into what discipline does each of the following departments fall?

Biology _____

Anthropology _____

Physics _____

Economics _____

Philosophy _____

Agronomy _____

History _____

Sociology _____

In what departments might you find information about the following topics?

Is bilingual education necessary? _____

What is the history of blues and jazz music? _____

Is cloning ethical? _____

Do all of these departments fall into the same disciplines? _____

how to select the keywords that will allow them to successfully locate information relating to their topic/question. Once the keywords have been selected, students should learn how to use a variety of terms with Boolean operators (AND, OR, NOT) to create a search string that will provide them with the specific information they are looking for.

Goal: Exercise 15 will help students identify concepts, keywords, terms, and synonyms of the words that will become their first round of search terms. They will also learn about Boolean operators and how they can make a search more successful.

Description: Students will use the instructor-provided "Search Term Worksheet" that follows to develop a list of concept terms related to the topic idea developed during concept mapping.

As the topic to be researched becomes clearer, more specific tools can be used to identify sources of information about the topic. Both print and online resources should be used. The concept of time sensitivity of some issues must be stressed. For example, the bulk of the information about the assassination of President John F. Kennedy was written in the 1960s and 1970s. Students may find little or nothing on the topic in the current literature. They must be advised and encouraged to leave the electronic environment if necessary to find information about their topic.

Students should also be advised that there may be parts of larger works that apply to their topics. A single chapter in a book or a single section in a book of proceedings might be useful, even though the entire book of proceedings is not.

Once the general information has been acquired, it is time to revise the topic. Is it too broad? Is it too narrow? Are there resources that will answer the question? What does the student need to know? Where are the answers most likely to be located?

Information literacy strives to give students a process that they can follow, a step-by-step instruction manual of sorts, to lay out the logical progression of steps to answer any information need. In teaching the research process, we lay out the steps for students and have them practice those steps one at a time.

Tip for conducting the exercise: We suggest having several dictionaries and thesauri in either online or print format available for students to consult during this exercise.

This exercise addresses ACRL Standard 1, Performance Indicator 1, and Standard 2, Performance Indicator 2.

Creating a Research Question

The table below illustrates how a research question develops from a broad topic to a focused question. Follow the four examples down the columns to see how the questions develop. Then use the blank form provided below to develop your own research question.

BROAD TOPIC	RESTRICTED TOPIC	NARROWED TOPIC	RESEARCH QUESTION
Pollution	Acid rain	Acid rain in the United States	What can the United States do to prevent acid rain?
Fishing	Commercial fishing	Fishing regulations and New England	What impact do fishing regulations have on commercial fishing in New England?
Censorship	Internet	Internet and China	How will China's effort to censor the Internet affect its citizens?
Nutrition	Diets	Vegetarianism	What nutritional benefits are there to vegetarianism?

Now try out your topic idea below. It is useful to work out several variations of the topic idea to see how it could change slightly and be improved or amended.

BROAD TOPIC	RESTRICTED TOPIC	NARROWED TOPIC	RESEARCH QUESTION

What type of question did you design?

❑ Comparison

❑ Cause and effect

❑ Measuring

❑ Process

Check to be sure that the research question meets these criteria:

❑ It is open-ended (cannot be answered with simple yes or no).

❑ It addresses an issue or controversy and/or solves a problem.

❑ It is something that you can take a stand on.

Search Term Worksheet

Search Question: Write down the research question you have developed. (Example: What is the connection between smoking and depression among teenagers?)

Major Concepts: List as many as apply. (Example: smoking, depression, teenagers)

The terms *AND, OR,* and *NOT* have a very specific use in online searching. These terms are called Boolean operators. They are used to direct computer software to perform certain functions. Using AND between two terms asks the computer to look for both terms in the same record. Using OR asks the computer to look for all records having either term. NOT tells the computer to ignore any record containing a term. Using Boolean operators allows you to give very specific instructions about what you want the computer to do. This will save you a lot of time you would otherwise spend sorting through records that are not useful to you.

Use the chart below to help you figure out some search terms.

CONCEPT 1		CONCEPT 2		CONCEPT 3
smoking		depression		teenagers
OR		OR		OR
cigarettes		mental health		teens
OR		OR		OR
tobacco	AND	mood	AND	adolescents
OR				OR
nicotine				youth
				OR
				high school students
				OR
				college students

Search Question: Write down the research question you have developed. Use the chart below to help you figure out some search terms.

Major Concepts: List as many as apply.

CONCEPT 1		CONCEPT 2		CONCEPT 3
OR		OR		OR
OR		OR		OR
	AND		AND	
OR		OR		OR
OR		OR		OR
OR		OR		OR

Chapter Four
The Chain of Information

As we have mentioned before, we are bombarded with information from numerous sources every single day. How is this information created? Whose creative powers have come into play to produce the information we get?

WHERE DOES INFORMATION COME FROM?

Most information comes to us through a process we call the information cycle. Here is an example. Jane has an idea. Jane gathers information from others about the idea. She talks about the idea with others—at home, at work, at the local baseball game—and gets feedback and input from others about the idea. For the idea to become a reality and for information about the idea to reach others, discussions become increasingly more focused to include experts and other people knowledgeable about the field into which the idea fits. Jane puts her idea in writing. This writing may be a conference paper, a proposal to her boss, or a letter to a company that might produce her idea as a new product. Once the idea is in writing, it gets passed around and discussed again. Jane might receive feedback from others to improve or modify her idea or to confirm the idea's validity. The writing might then be translated into a project proposal, or a patent, or a manuscript to be published in a scholarly journal. If it appears that more information is available to be gathered and compiled, one idea might become a book or a group of products.

The next person, John, might read Jane's book and get a new idea, which will start the information cycle over again.

HOW DO WE RECEIVE INFORMATION?

Information comes to us from different sources at different times. For example, as events are taking place, they are usually reported in spoken format during a news broadcast over the radio, television, or Internet. This can happen literally while the event is occurring or only moments after. Most of the information in this kind of report is sketchy and includes only very basic facts (who, what, where, when).

With the advent of widespread Internet access, breaking news is increasingly reported in text or video over the Internet (or via such short message services as Twitter) at about the same time as the live radio and television news broadcasts are taking place. Within a day of the event, its description will appear in daily publications such as newspapers. Again, the information will be general and focus on the bare facts, although there may have been enough time to collect some additional information (background about geographic locations, identity of people involved, brief history of a problem).

After a few days, the event will appear in weekly newsmagazines. A magazine article on the event will provide broader coverage, which might include a number of sidebars discussing related topics. There may be more details and even some coverage of the "whys" surrounding an event. These articles are written by staff members who work for the newsmagazine. These authors may or may not be experts on their assigned topics. A newsmagazine does not usually list the sources of its information. Most newsmagazine articles are not allotted enough space to discuss the deeper meanings or possible consequences of a particular event. This type of reporting is usually continued in magazines that are published less frequently, if the event is relevant to the scope of the magazine.

In three to six months, articles will begin to appear in scholarly literature. These articles tend to be written by people who are experts in the field under discussion. The articles can be lengthy and attempt to cover the topic in depth. Many facts will be included along with the analysis of those facts, history of the topic in this particular case and in general, and the possible consequences of the event.

In one to three years, books will appear about the topic. There are many different types of books published for many different types of audiences. All books are lengthy documents. It takes time to compile enough information to create a book. Books can be written by experts or nonexperts. They can be scholarly or popular. They may include a bibliography or not.

Finally, if the topic was of enough interest or had significant impact, a brief outline of the event will appear in a reference tool such as an encyclopedia.

INFORMATION AND THE EFFECTS OF TIME

Different kinds of publications are published on different schedules, which impacts the depth and breadth of information provided by the publication. Daily publications like newspapers are limited by the time frame they have to do the reporting. Book authors can take more time to develop ideas, do research, and write in depth on their topic.

Goal: Exercise 16 will allow students to understand the kinds of information they might find during, just after, and long after a significant event. It will also provide practice in the identification and location of different sources of information about the same event.

Description: Students will work in teams of two or three. The instructor will pass out index cards on which are written the name of a significant event and its date. Students will be asked to find the first citation

Exercise 16

Information and Time

You will work in twos or threes. You will be given an index card with a brief description of an event and the date of this event. Working together, find the earliest citation to information about the event in a newspaper, a magazine, a scholarly journal, and a book. Write the complete citations on the worksheet. Then think about the questions below and be ready to discuss them.

Newspaper article: _____
_____

Magazine: _____
_____

Scholarly journal: _____
_____

Book: _____
_____

What kind of publication was the first to supply information about the event?

What kind of publication took the longest to supply information about the event?

What kind of publication would you consider to be the most reliable and authoritative in supplying this information? Why?

for a newspaper article, a magazine article, a scholarly journal article, and a book about this event.

Tips for conducting the exercise: We found that events about ten years in the past provided the best results. With increasing rates of publication in electronic format, it may not always be necessary to identify events that far in the past. Students may need assistance in locating indexes that will cover their event. For example, they may need to go to a paper index rather than using an online index with an inadequate date range for coverage. Students could answer the questions during class discussion or as an assignment outside of class.

This exercise addresses ACRL Standard 2.

HOW RESEARCH METHODS DEVELOP

Research has been refined over a long period of time so that it can build upon itself rather than requiring each researcher to start from zero. Before the invention of the printing press, information was located in specific places or with specific people. It was possible for people to share their ideas with others on a very limited basis and scale. Many people did not read or write, and those who did were widely scattered. Information that was written down had to be copied by hand in order to share it with someone not able to get to the location of the original document.

With the invention of the printing press in 1436, the use of information changed over a relatively short period of time. Books, pamphlets, and other types of publications still took a long time to produce, but this mechanical means of producing any number of copies of the same information allowed that information to be shared widely. This meant that existing information could be printed and disseminated, allowing the thinkers of the day to build on the work done in the existing document rather than reinventing the idea from scratch. Printing also made the cost of owning a printed item much more affordable.

Because it was so much easier to get written information, it became much more necessary to become literate. After the invention of the printing press, many more people saw incentive, even necessity, in being able to read.

As literacy and the availability of written information increased, it became increasingly necessary to keep track of the authorship of each document.

Knowing who wrote something allowed a researcher to contact the author to ask questions, share insights, or verify the information. Authors wanted others to know that they, and no other, had written some piece of information.

Over a long period of time, it became customary to acknowledge authorship of works cited in one's own publications rather than waiting for someone to ask, "Who wrote that?" The custom of listing works cited became the footnotes, endnotes, and bibliography citations researchers use today. In this way, new researchers could show others that they had read all or part of what was already in writing about a particular topic while introducing new material of their own. Rather than repeating what others said, a new author could simply refer a reader to the other materials of relevance. Needless to say, this saved much time and effort for everyone involved.

For research purposes today, it is usual to start with the most current information on a topic and work backward. But how?

There are several methods for working backward through time to collect information about a topic. One method relies on the researcher having a written piece of information in hand. It may be the current issue of a scholarly publication, a new book, a current newspaper article, or an Internet website.

In the publication that the researcher has in hand resides a list of sources that the author used to support his or her thesis. This list, which most often appears at the end of a book or scholarly paper, is called a bibliography. It is supplied so that the reader may refer to those other publications. It can tell a knowledgeable reader whether the author has carried out a good search of the existing literature. It can provide the author with credibility by showing that he or she has considered the range of opinion about the question.

The bibliography is also a list of publications about the same topic in which the researcher is interested. By looking at the list of publications in the bibliography of a new book or scholarly article, the reader has a number of other sources about the same topic identified. When looking at a copy of each of the publications in a new bibliography, a researcher can collect additional sources about the same topic from the bibliographies of those books and journal articles. Each of the second set of publications will have a bibliography that will refer to relevant and older materials. Researchers have access to an expanding pyramid of sources of information about a particular topic by identifying one appropriate article, using the items in its bibliography to identify other appropriate articles, selecting items in the bibliographies of those articles to identify still more items of interest, and so on. This chain of information theoretically extends back to the original writing done on the topic.

Exercise 17

Links in the Chain of Information

For this exercise we will begin by looking at a current article on a topic. Attached to that article is a bibliography. This is a list of publications about the same topic that were used by the author of the current article to create it.

From that bibliographic list, note that two citations are marked. Imagine that you are a researcher. You might scan the bibliography of a current article to find other articles on the same topic. The two citations marked are the citations of interest to you in your role as the imaginary researcher.

> What would you do to get a copy of these publications? (Online catalog search, interlibrary loan, Union List search, and so on.)

Now we have copies of those two publications. Each of them has a bibliography of its own. Continuing in your role as researcher, select two more citations from each of these bibliographies.

> To obtain copies of these four publications, what would you do?

Now that you have received copies of these four publications, you find that each one has its own bibliography. Note that two items from each of these bibliographies have been marked for selection. If you get copies of each of these publications, you will have fifteen articles about your research topic.

> What do you notice about the publication dates as we continue?

> How far back in time could we go using this method?

THE CHAIN OF INFORMATION

It is important for a researcher to know who provided information, at what time in the chain of events, and with how much background knowledge. It is also important to follow the chain of information to see how a topic has developed over time as well as to benefit from the research work already done by others concerning the same topic.

Goal: For exercise 17 students begin with a scholarly work and by using its bibliography work backward in time to re-create part of the chain of information about that topic.

Description: Students will be given a copy of a scholarly article. They will examine the bibliography attached to the article and select two citations. Then the student will locate the publications cited and examine those bibliographies. Two citations will be selected from each of those bibliographies. The student now has four new citations. The four new publications will be located, and the bibliographies for those publications will be examined. Two citations will be selected from each of those bibliographies. This procedure might be followed one additional step before becoming too cumbersome.

Tips for conducting the exercise: Although it might be possible to do this exercise in small groups, unless one has access to a very large and very comprehensive library (or one that specializes in the selected topic), it may be hard to get an actual copy of the articles selected from the bibliographies. This exercise works best if the instructor selects the citations from the publications before class and already has them on hand for the class. Information could be put on overheads for demonstration purposes.

This exercise addresses ACRL Standard 2, Performance Indicators 3 and 5.

Chapter Five

Issues of the Information Age

Information has been around for a long time. The issues in using, storing, retrieving, and sharing information have always been with us. Copyright, privacy, and fair use have been debated for centuries. Something like consensus about standard practice has emerged in the United States concerning these topics. However, in the era of the Internet, with all its new technologies, these issues surface again. New formats, new ease of access, and new applications all require that the issues surrounding the use of information be revisited.

QUANTITY OF INFORMATION

The sheer amount of information that exists is staggering. The availability of this information to the general public has created a new set of problems. Should everyone be able to see all the information that exists? Should everyone be able to use that information, and, if so, how? What happens when the government needs information about an individual? What happens when one individual wants information about someone else? How do you know where "virtual" information comes from? How does one sort out the good information from the bad information? How does one know what is good? How does one find the time to select and evaluate a few sources from among the huge number of possible sources? The mechanisms for delivering information are also expanding in number and in scope. We have moved from the spoken word to the written word and have arrived in a place where we can have information in just about any format geared for any one or more of our senses.

The speed at which information moves is also increasing. Information that used to be transmitted in a haphazard manner by word of mouth can now be delivered specifically, accurately, and in many different formats to any number of people, anywhere on the globe, and sometimes into outer space.

In all this information-centered chaos in the new information age, there are new ways of looking at almost every information issue.

INTELLECTUAL PROPERTY

In earlier stages of the information age, it was fairly simple to assign intellectual property rights to the appropriate person. You wrote an original story, you put your name on the title page, and it was yours. Today, things are not so simple. Information is offered anonymously. Information is offered by groups affiliated with some institution or on their own. Information is easy to borrow, cut and paste, link to, and modify. Some information is freely available. Other information costs money. How then do we make sense of intellectual property?

Authorship

What is an author? Before the time of computers, an author was usually someone who wrote something on paper. It might be words, it might be music, or it might be mathematical calculations. Today, people still become authors in the traditional way. There are also many new technologies people use to create something that makes them authors. For example, in the scientific community an idea might occur to a number of different people who will "toss it around" with other colleagues all over the world via the Internet. As the idea takes shape through this collaborative process, it becomes difficult to identify an owner of the intellectual property. There are really many authors. The property belongs to the scientific community at large. This is a concept that is difficult to codify. When information about this scientific idea is published, who gets the credit?

When information comes up on an Internet website, it is extremely difficult to know where it came from. In a "cut-and-paste" environment, any piece of information could come from almost anywhere. It could be that the author of web page A gathered ideas from web pages B, C, and D. Those pages may or may not have identified their authors. The information on web pages B, C, and D may have been swiped, borrowed, or paraphrased from other web pages, other kinds of documents, or other kinds of communications. It is very easy to lose track of authorship on the Internet, where pages come and go, links come and go, and where anyone can post anything he or she likes. Authors would be hard-pressed to keep track of their ideas and monitor who is using them for what purpose in the virtual environment. It follows that it is much more difficult to protect the rights of authors in the virtual environment.

Today, the word *author* can apply to many people in situations that might never have existed twenty years ago. Is the person who develops a computer program that is stored on the hard drive of a computer an author? Is someone who makes a videotape an author? Is someone who takes a digital image and manipulates it to create something different an author? If all of these people are authors, then they should all be protected under the laws that protect traditional authors. Or should they?

WHAT IS AN AUTHOR?

Many students have never considered what it feels like to be an author. They have never looked at the ownership rights of an author from that point of view. It is common in the current electronic environment to use someone else's work as a starting point for one's own. For example, many nonprofessional designers of websites are willing to allow others to copy their layouts, color schemes, hot links, and so on. Students will find a website whose looks they like and copy it or copy and modify it to suit their own needs. One of the original reasons for the popularity of the Internet was the ability to share, to dispense with the need to reinvent the wheel, and to be able to build on the gains that others made previously.

It is important to remind students, however, that credit must be given to the creators of any intellectual property—whether it be ideas or words or programming or images—if it is used in an academic assignment. This is necessary so that others can recreate the trail the student followed in doing his or her research. It is necessary so that individual sources can be accessed for verification or for use by other researchers. It is necessary so that the person who did the original work gets credit for it.

Goal: Exercise 18 allows students to put themselves in the author's shoes and consider from that point of view what it means to be an author and what an author's rights are.

Description: Divide the class into small groups. Discuss the worksheet questions and jot down ideas. Reconvene the class for a large group discussion. Role-play the plight of an author who discovers that someone is using his or her work without permission and earning lots of money for it.

Tip for conducting the exercise: It is useful to have other instructors who have rehearsed the role-play do the skit for the large group discussion.

This exercise addresses ACRL Standard 5.

Authorship, Rights of Authors, and Responsible Use of Others' Work

In small groups, discuss the following questions and record your best answers.

What or who is an author? What does it mean to create something?

Are you an author? Name some of the things you have created.

Suppose you wrote a prizewinning essay about information literacy. You win a certificate and a handshake from the dean of your college. Then you find out that your roommate sent your essay to a magazine essay contest with his or her name on it instead of yours. Your roommate wins $5,000 and a spot on a popular TV show. How do you feel about what just happened? What can you do about what your roommate did?

Suppose your roommate took only one paragraph of your essay and still won the money and the TV experience. Would you feel any differently?

Suppose your roommate took your ideas, changed the language just a little, and won the money. Now how do you feel?

What is plagiarism?

Why is it important to cite your sources (tell others whose intellectual property you used) when writing or doing other kinds of research? List all the possible reasons you can think of.

Does participation in peer-to-peer file-sharing services count as a form of plagiarism or not? Does it infringe on the copyrights of authors or creators?

INFORMATION LITERACY FORUMS

Contributed by Jim Kinnie

Too often information literacy exercises narrowly focus on research for academic papers when in fact lifelong learning is a goal of a good information literacy program. Many students don't realize that information literacy skills are just as important in their postgraduate lives as they are during their academic careers. One way to reinforce this idea is to interact with professionals in various fields who use information literacy skills in their daily work lives. The following describes how to produce an information-issues forum that will bring professionals and students together for a discussion of using information literacy skills after graduation.

The forum is ideal for a lesson in a credit-bearing information literacy course, but it can be scaled to fit many situations. It can be a promotional vehicle for the library's status on campus or for a collaborative effort with other departments such as journalism, writing, biological or medical sciences, and business and marketing; just about any discipline will use information literacy skills in its profession. The forum can take place in a classroom, a large meeting room, or an auditorium. The audience can be limited to one section

of a course or can be open to the campus community and the public at large.

Goal: In exercise 19, students will gain an understanding of how the evaluative skills and ethical use of information as outlined in the ACRL standards can be applied in a nonacademic setting. They will learn how evaluating information can make a real difference in business, government, health, consumer, and legal decisions and how those decisions affect people's lives and careers.

Description: The forum can take many forms, and the topic can be one that is a subject of debate in the community or anything that might have an impact on students' lives. It can tie in with an event that has a national focus—like Sunshine Week, in the spring, or Banned Books Week, in the fall—or it can have a more personal focus, like illegal file sharing or Facebook privacy issues. A contentious political season is a good time to evaluate facts presented in political advertisements. Several examples follow.

Scenario 1: Panel Discussion. Assemble a panel of three to four professionals who work in fields relating to the main topic. For example, a forum on censorship could include an art museum director, a civil liberties lawyer, and a religious leader; a forum on fact-checking in the news media provides an opportunity for producers, editors, or reporters from media outlets such as newspapers, television, and blogs to share their experiences; a discussion of privileged information could include a federal prosecutor, a scientist, and a journalist, who could discuss the implications of secret information, national security letters, business research, and Freedom of Information Act requests. Any of these panels could also include a faculty member from an appropriate department to give an academic perspective on the topic.

Each panelist is given fifteen to twenty minutes to present his or her perspective on the topic. Presenters air their opinions, which, depending on their positions, could be set up as opposing viewpoints or as unconventional perspectives on the topic. The forum

Exercise 19

Expert Input on Information Issues

Before the forum, you will prepare questions for panelists based on your knowledge of the topic. Research the topic using the online catalog, periodical databases, and websites to find information that will outline the controversy, explain the issues, and explore the panelists' backgrounds. Be prepared to fully engage them in the discussion. A question-and-answer period after the presentations will give you the opportunity to ask your questions.

After the forum is over, you will have one week to write a reaction paper. Summarize the topic of the forum and give your impressions of the panelists and their messages in a two-page essay. Include your reactions, positive and negative, to the ideas presented and how you will personally apply any lessons learned.

is then opened up to the audience for a question-and-answer period. A moderator (an outgoing librarian, a local news personality or radio talk-show host, a subject faculty member) selects the questioners and keeps the discussion on topic.

Scenario 2: Game Show. There are many models of game shows that can be adapted—*Jeopardy! Who Wants to Be a Millionaire? What's My Line?*—or one can be created to fit a theme. For instance, a forum on intellectual property involves using a PowerPoint slide show identifying examples of plagiarism, fabrication, and fair use in real life. Contestants are recruited or chosen at random from the audience to form competing teams. Excerpts from recent books, popular music-sampling clips, or legal decisions are displayed, and contestants decide if they violate intellectual property principles or not. A "celebrity" panel of faculty, lawyers, artists, editors, or those in related disciplines discusses the example and concurs or disagrees with the contestants. Points are awarded, and the highest-scoring team wins prizes, which could be as inexpensive as candy bars.

Scenario 3: Media Presentation/Panel. This format works well with any controversial use of media, but it can be particularly engaging during an election year. The forum uses political advertisements that are organized around themes of negative advertising, positive biographical expositions, factual inaccuracies, and so forth, and shown to the audience for their reaction. Ads are shown individually or in groups, with frequent pauses for audience reaction and discussion. A faculty member in political science and/or a local political reporter guides the discussion to give a real-world perspective on the effects of the ads.

Those in the audience who usually do not pay much attention to politics will be drawn into this unique art of persuasion and may begin to realize the consequences of not critically evaluating political messages.

Tips for conducting the exercise: The setup for the forum will take the most energy and effort. Choosing and contacting potential guests, arranging the location,

publicizing the event, and addressing a myriad of other considerations will take the most time. The forum can be fit into an hour and a half to two hours, and any follow-up sessions with students will vary depending on the context.

The topic and panelists should be chosen with audience interest in mind. A local event or something in the news that has captured national attention and has local implications, a campus controversy, and theme celebrations like those mentioned above will foster lively discussions. It's important to choose the right speakers. Many local organizations would be happy to oblige and help their own cause along with enlightening students. News reporters, scientists, consumer advocates, artists—all are generally great information evaluators and are often dynamic presenters. Panelists can be recruited from within your institution, in the wider world, and referrals from family and friends. Using your (and your colleagues') personal contacts is a good way to assemble a panel without the high price of contracting a nationally recognized speaker.

Your institution's culture and policies will determine the best time and place for the forum. Beware of conflicts with other events or time slots that restrict audience participation. The venue you choose should fit the audience—not too big or too small—and should have the required technology. The budget is scalable also depending on expenses like providing dinner or an honoraria for speakers, advertising in local media, and printing costs for programs and flyers. Communication is a key consideration for success; press releases, interviews with campus media outlets, or invitations to local media will spread the word about the event. See the checklist of forum-preparation activities in figure 5.1.

Following the forum event, and to further explore a topic, students may work in groups and use library resources to investigate different aspects of the subject to verify or refute the information they discovered in the forum. Group presentations should follow to give a wide perspective on the theme of the forum.

If the forum is a library event on campus, librarians can work with subject faculty to design related activities for their classes that attended.

The important thing is to tie the forum topic to students' lives outside of school. It should raise the consciousness of students so they will see that taking a critical look at the information they see, read, and hear throughout their lives is just as important, if not more so, than deciding on the information they use in a research paper.

An in-class means of discussing issues of the information age is helpful when time does not permit an issues-forum presentation. Exercise 20 fits into the context of one or two classroom sessions.

This exercise addresses ACRL Standard 3, Performance Indicator 4; and Standard 5, Performance Indicator 2.

Figure 5.1

INFORMATION ISSUES FORUM CHECKLIST

THREE MONTHS IN ADVANCE
- ❏ Brainstorm with staff and/or faculty
- ❏ Pick a topic
- ❏ Pick a title
- ❏ Identify and invite speakers
- ❏ Identify and invite a moderator
- ❏ Pick a date
- ❏ Invite speakers
- ❏ Create a budget
  - ❏ Advertising
  - ❏ Printing
  - ❏ Food

TWO TO THREE MONTHS IN ADVANCE
- ❏ Schedule space
- ❏ Reserve equipment
- ❏ Reserve dinner
- ❏ Secure funding

TWO TO FOUR WEEKS IN ADVANCE
- ❏ Notify appropriate faculty
- ❏ Create flyers
- ❏ Write press releases
- ❏ Schedule printing
- ❏ Secure parking passes
- ❏ Update speakers
  - ❏ Clarify topic
  - ❏ Answer questions

- ❏ Request bios for program
- ❏ Keep them happy

ONE TO TWO WEEKS IN ADVANCE
- ❏ Personally contact on- and off-campus participants
- ❏ Double-check:
  - ❏ Space
  - ❏ Equipment
  - ❏ Press releases
  - ❏ Dinner reservations
- ❏ Create programs
- ❏ Buy advertisements (campus newspaper or radio)
- ❏ Place announcement on campus and library websites
- ❏ Distribute flyers on campus (printing services) and off campus (academic and public libraries)

FORUM DAY
- ❏ Put up signage
- ❏ Set the stage
- ❏ Test equipment
- ❏ Provide water for speakers

ONE WEEK FOLLOWING
- ❏ Send thank-you notes
- ❏ Evaluate the forum

ISSUES OF THE INFORMATION AGE

The proliferation of information has created a new set of concerns for everyone. Privacy, accuracy, intellectual property rights, ownership, and censorship are examples of areas of great concern. Students should be aware of these issues and what is at stake for them as global citizens.

Goal: Students often don't realize that there may be problems associated with access to information. Exercise 20 helps to inform them about the problems and how students might be impacted by those issues.

Description: Students are divided into small groups. Each group is given an "issue" to investigate. The group members will find three or four articles about their issue that help explain what the issue is and why we should care about it. The group should discuss the issue and create a five-minute presentation, skit, or other creative activity about the issue. Each group will create a bibliography of the articles reviewed and submit it to the instructor.

Issues we have identified are courtesy cards or loyalty cards at supermarkets, drugstores, and so forth; radio frequency identification (RFID) tags in purchased items; spyware/adware/cookies; copyright; video surveillance or social-networking sites; violations of Internet policies; and plagiarism. We created a scenario for each issue to put the issue into context for the students. For example:

Loyalty cards: When you go to many stores, cashiers frequently ask you if you have your courtesy or loyalty card. Companies use these cards to keep track of you, your purchases, and more. How much do these companies know about you? What are they doing with the information?

RFID: Walmart and other retailers are embedding RFID tags in items they sell to track inventory, but the chips still work long after you leave the store. What is RFID, and what might it mean for you?

Video surveillance: A recent Kenneth Cole ad campaign states, "You are on a video camera an average of 10 times a day. Are you dressed for it?" Surveillance cameras installed after 9/11 caught the bus that dumped sewage on Chicago tourists, and recently mounted cameras catch those who run red lights at many city intersections. Are we becoming a surveillance society? Who can put a camera up, and what happens to the tapes?

Tips for conducting the exercise: You may want to give groups class time to work on this assignment so that they have time to identify quality articles and read them. You may also make this a multiclass assignment.

This exercise addresses ACRL Standards 1, 2, 3, 4, and 5.

Publisher

What is a publisher? Back in the day of paper-only publishing, a publisher was a company with employees

---

Exercise 20

Marketing, Security, Inventory, or Invasion of Privacy?

For this assignment, you and your group will present an important issue of the information age to the class. Once you have your assigned "issue," find three or four articles on the topic. Articles must be two pages or longer and must be of good quality. Use your searching and evaluation skills to help you find good articles.

- Read the articles, and discuss them with your group.

- Work together to create a five-minute presentation, skit, or other creative activity about the issue.

- The basic questions you should address in your presentation follow:

  - What is the issue? Imagine that we know nothing about the topic.
  - What are the pros and cons of the issue?
  - Should we care? Why or why not? What importance does this issue have on our lives?

- Finally, designate someone to make a quick bibliography to show what sources you used. This should be in correct MLA format, with the group members' names on it. Hand it in when you present your issue.

For this assignment, use databases that have full-text articles available in them. You may also want to go to the Electronic Privacy Information Center (EPIC) website, at www.epic.org, for information on your issue.

who oversaw the transformation of a book from a manuscript to a printed volume that could be mass-produced. The publisher had editors, artists, typesetters, printers, and binders to accomplish this task. Publishers produced approximately 550,000 books by these methods in 2008.

Today, anyone can be a publisher. All that is required is access to a computer that has access to the Internet. An author can be his or her own publisher. An author may have his or her writing published in paper or electronic format. A writer may have works published by someone unknown to him or her, with or without permission.

Publishing in electronic format has some distinct advantages. Traditional methods of publication are time-consuming, while electronic publishing can take only a matter of minutes. Information published on paper reaches only those who care to buy the published work or visit a library that has purchased the book. Electronic publication potentially puts the writing into the hands of millions of Internet users—at least in theory.

However, the electronic environment is not without its drawbacks. Self-publishing or electronic publishing through someone else may not include the editorial assistance and expertise of a traditional publisher. The layout, the language, and the presentation of the work may receive little or no expert attention if self-published. The millions of potential readers of electronic books may not be required to pay for access to the work, or the content might be copied from a restricted site and placed on an unrestricted site by some savvy hacker. This does not work well for the author and publisher seeking fortune rather than fame. In the electronic environment, it is also relatively simple to cut and paste one author's writing and attribute it to someone else, effectively eliminating any rights the author or publisher might have to the content—at least until the matter is settled through the court system. Again, it is very difficult in the virtual book business for an author or a publisher to keep track of how a work is being modified and by whom. It is not economically feasible for a publisher to prosecute every misuse of electronically mounted intellectual property, even though protections of the owners' rights exist.

Copyright

Copyright refers to the legal right to reproduce, publish, and sell intellectual property. In many cases, the author holds the copyright. This means that the author is the only person who can publish and sell his or her work. An author may give permission for someone else to publish a work without giving up the copyright.

Many times the copyright is held jointly by the author and the publisher. Thus, they share the right to reproduce, publish, or sell the work. This is beneficial to both parties. It assists the author by placing the resources and the name of the publisher before the reader. This can result in increased sales for an unknown author if the publisher has a widely known name and a reputation for publishing good books. Should the author need to enforce copyright by suing, the publisher would be likely to have more resources available for that purpose. The publisher benefits from joint copyright by receiving a portion of the sales revenues.

Sometimes the author assigns the copyright to the publisher entirely. The author may receive a negotiated royalty for every book or journal sold but will no longer own the right to reproduce, publish, or sell the item him- or herself. Any legal considerations regarding the copyright in this case are the sole responsibility of the publisher. The publisher usually receives all or most of the sales receipts and does not have to get the author's permission to change the cover design or the layout.

An institution may also hold a copyright. Just as the patent for an invention created on the job may belong to the company, the copyright on intellectual products created on work time may belong to the institution paying the salary of the author. In this case, the institution reaps the benefits and bears the burdens of holding the copyright.

The Digital Millennium Copyright Act, passed by Congress in 1998, was created to extend copyright protections into the digital and electronic environments.

Fair Use

Copyright law is written to protect the owners of the copyright from loss of potential income. There are some provisions that apply to special situations to allow the copyright holders' rights to take a backseat. One of these provisions is known as fair use. Fair use spells out when and how non–copyright holders can use copyrighted material. For example, a photocopy of a journal article may be made for educational purposes as long as the copy is not sold for profit. This allows researchers to do their work without having to bear an unmanageable cost for doing so. It allows research to move forward without having to wait for the copyright holder's permission to copy the material. A teacher may make a copy of something to use as an example in a classroom, to help students learn a concept, idea, painting style, and so on. Fair use provisions are there to allow research, scientific, and scholarly progress to go forward without hampering the copyright holder's right to sell the item.

Plagiarism

Plagiarism is the technical term for stealing someone else's intellectual property. If students cut and paste something created by someone else and do not give credit to the creator, they are plagiarizing. In colleges, universities, and research institutions, plagiarism can cause big problems. Many institutions have very strict guidelines and punishments for those who plagiarize. The electronic environment has changed the way people use information and has made it very difficult to attribute credit to the creator and very easy to borrow the information without attribution.

PLAGIARISM AND HOW TO AVOID IT

Many students, especially those versed in the cut-and-paste world of the computer, do not understand what plagiarism is. Some have vague notions about not using the exact words of others, but for the most part students are unsure about what they must cite. Students may know that they may use information that is common knowledge without attribution, but most have no clear idea of what "common knowledge" is. Students tend to think about quoting, citing, and plagiarizing only with reference to traditional sources of academic knowledge—books and journals. They need to be encouraged to think about other sources of information and how it is protected as well.

Goal: The goal of exercise 21 is to identify instances of plagiarism and to learn what can be changed in each selection to make each passage acceptable to use.

Description: This exercise contains a quotation from a document. The quotation is followed by examples that use the exact words of the passage, that paraphrase the passage, and that use small parts of the passage with and without quotation marks and with and without attribution. This exercise is designed to show specific

examples of plagiarism. Students should be able to identify what is missing from the writing or what needs to be done to correct the error.

Tips for conducting the exercise: This exercise works well with individuals, with small groups, or as a whole-group discussion. If the group is divided, be sure to bring students back together to discuss each example and to compare notes on their conclusions.

This exercise addresses ACRL Standard 5.

REAL-LIFE PLAGIARISM AND WHAT IT COSTS

There is nothing like real life to bring the issue of plagiarism home to a student. This plagiarism exercise looks at a real-life example.

Goal: In exercise 22, students will learn how plagiarism can occur and how it can change a life by following the events as they happened and discussing ethical issues surrounding the events.

Description: The instructor will tell the story of Kaavya Viswanathan and her book, *How Opal Mehta Got Kissed, Got Wild, and Got a Life.* Have students take a few minutes to read articles giving the details of the story. Divide the class into small groups. Have each group select a moderator, recorder, and spokesperson. Give the groups ten to fifteen minutes to discuss and record responses to the questions they received. After the time for discussion has ended, ask each group spokesperson to report to the class on the group's answers to the questions.

Use these culminating questions with the entire class after each group reports on the group questions:

1. What effect can plagiarism have on someone's life? How do you imagine it could impact your own life?

2. What does "internalizing" what was read previously mean? Have you ever experienced it?

3. Why is plagiarism wrong?

Wrap up the class discussion by having students discuss ways to prevent plagiarizing thoughts and ideas in academic life and in everyday situations.

Tips for conducting the exercise: Consider adding details to the story of Viswanathan's plagiarism if time and interest warrant. After sharing the story, show an actual copy of the book or demonstrate a search in

Plagiarism

The quotation below is from an article by Joanna M. Burkhardt. Read the original quotation. Selections 1 through 7 are ways in which someone might use this information in a term paper. Which of these constitute plagiarism, and which are acceptable? Compare the examples that follow, and decide whether they are or are not examples of plagiarism. Be ready to explain your answer. Original quotation:

> Library literature offers wide-spectrum coverage on planning and moving libraries. Authors offer visions of what might be, practical implementation suggestions, or explicit instructions for specific situations. Every move is different and offers its own set of challenges. Planning and moving into a new library can be a nightmare with long-range challenges, or a sweet dream of perfect coordination and timing.*

Selection 1
Library literature offers wide-spectrum coverage on planning and moving libraries. Authors offer visions of what might be, practical implementation suggestions, or explicit instructions for specific situations. Every move is different and offers its own set of challenges. Planning and moving into a new library can be a nightmare with long-range challenges, or a sweet dream of perfect coordination and timing.

Selection 2
Library literature offers wide-spectrum coverage on planning and moving libraries. Authors offer visions of what might be, practical implementation suggestions, or explicit instructions for specific situations. Every move is different and offers its own set of challenges. Planning and moving into a new library can be a nightmare with long-range challenges, or a sweet dream of perfect coordination and timing. (Burkhardt, 1998)

Selection 3
"Library literature offers wide-spectrum coverage on planning and moving libraries. Authors offer visions of what might be, practical implementation suggestions, or explicit instructions for specific situations. Every move is different and offers its own set of challenges. Planning and moving into a new library can be a nightmare with long-range challenges or a sweet dream of perfect coordination and timing." (Burkhardt, 1998)

Selection 4
Library literature offers much information on planning and moving libraries. Authors offer their thoughts on what might be, practical implementation suggestions, or explicit instructions for specific situations. Every move is different and offers its own set of challenges. Planning and moving into a new library can be a nightmare or a sweet dream of perfect coordination and timing. (Burkhardt, 1998)

Selection 5
"Library literature offers much information on planning and moving libraries. Authors offer their thoughts on what might be, practical implementation suggestions, or explicit instructions for specific situations. Every move is different and offers its own set of challenges. Planning and moving into a new library can be a nightmare or a sweet dream of perfect coordination and timing." (Burkhardt, 1998)

Selection 6
In the literature about libraries there are plenty of articles on planning and moving libraries. Writers of these articles offer futuristic, practical, or explicit instructions for moving libraries. Planning and moving a library can be a nightmare or a good dream. (Burkhardt, 1998)

Selection 7
Moving into a new library takes much planning and forethought. The literature is full of articles of practical and theoretical advice regarding this topic. Each situation is different and must be handled according to the specifics of the location. Creating a new library may be very easy or very hard. (Burkhardt, 1998)

*Joanna M. Burkhardt, "Do's and don'ts for moving a small academic library," *College and Research Libraries News* 59, no. 7 (July/August 1998): 499.

WorldCat or another large catalog to show that there are copies of this book available for reading. (As of this writing, per WorldCat, more than 680 libraries own the book *How Opal Mehta Got Kissed, Got Wild, and Got a Life*.) You might also show the students a photograph of Viswanathan to illustrate that she was just a college student (like they are now) when this happened.

The wrap-up discussion could simply be conversation in class, but you can add to it by creating a list of "best practices to prevent plagiarism" for the students and posting it on a class website or displaying it on a poster in the classroom.

This exercise addresses ACRL Standard 5.

Exercise 22

How Plagiarism Changed a Life

Let's look at a real-life example of plagiarism.

Kaavya Viswanathan was nineteen and a freshman at Harvard when she was offered a two-book deal of $500,000 to write "chick lit." Viswanathan wrote a book titled *How Opal Mehta Got Kissed, Got Wild, and Got a Life*. The book was published in April 2006, and it quickly became a best seller. DreamWorks bought the rights, planning to produce a film based on the book. Soon after it was published, however, reports of possible plagiarism surfaced. In the end, there were more than forty plagiarized passages identified in Viswanathan's novel. The book was pulled from store shelves April 27, 2006, and the book deal was canceled. Viswanathan apologized, saying that she "must have internalized" those details (from the other author's books) without realizing it. Viswanathan remained at Harvard despite the plagiarism event.

Read the two articles below.

> Story about Viswanathan in the *Harvard Crimson:* www.thecrimson.com/article. aspx?ref=512948

> Update on Viswanathan from—ye gads!— Wikipedia! http://en.wikipedia.org/wiki/ Kaavya_Viswanathan

The class will be divided into small discussion groups. Each group will discuss one question. Select a moderator, recorder, and spokesperson for your group. You will have ten to fifteen minutes to discuss and record your responses to the question you received. The spokesperson for each group will report to the class on the group's answers to the questions.

Questions

Group 1: If you were the author Meg Cabot, how would you feel about your ideas being stolen by Kaavya Viswanathan and used in *Opal Mehta*? If you were Viswanathan, would you apologize to the author? Why or why not?

Group 2: Why do you think Viswanathan plagiarized passages from the other chick lit author in her novel? Do you think that this case of plagiarism was intentional? What should the consequences be for plagiarizing in the publishing world?

Group 3: One student was interviewed about the *Opal Mehta* issue and said, "What difference does it make if [Viswanathan] wrote it or not? It's still a good book." How do you feel about this statement? What responsibility should the editor and publisher have with regard to verifying that their authors do not plagiarize?

Group 4: How are you going to be more aware of your writing and not plagiarize by citing sources in the future? What are the roles and responsibilities of a university community to ensure that students do not plagiarize for campus assignments? Is an "Honor Code and Pledge" adequate to ensure that students do not plagiarize? What should be the consequences of plagiarizing (e.g., failure of paper, failure of course, expulsion from the university)?

Group 5: If you were Viswanathan, would you have gone back to Harvard after this incident of plagiarism? Do you think Harvard should have expelled Viswanathan? Do you believe that Viswanathan's professors are going to treat her in the same respect as other students after this incident? Where do you think Kaavya Viswanathan is now, a few years after the controversy?

Adapted from an exercise created by Carrie A. Kelly, Librarian, St. George's School, Newport, Rhode Island.

When to Cite

How does a writer know when it is appropriate to cite someone else's work? The answer to this question is frequently unclear even for a practiced author. However, in each case, the writer must make a decision one way or the other—to cite or not to cite. Under the law, the only time it is acceptable not to cite a source for someone else's work is when the information under consideration is common knowledge. An author does not have to find the source for the information "The sun rises in the east." This fact is common knowledge. There are many facts that can be considered common knowledge.

The concept of common knowledge becomes a gray area when we begin to consider the question, Common to whom? It seems fair to assume that every adult knows that the sun rises in the east, wherever they are and whatever their culture. The certainty about what is common knowledge becomes less certain when issues are common to many, but not to all, people. For example, it is common knowledge for adults in the United States that cars drive on the right side of the road in the United States. This may not be common knowledge in other places on the globe. It may be common knowledge for those who work in the computer industry that Apple computers invented the concept of computer windows.[1] That information may not be common knowledge to those outside the industry.

One must be very careful about assuming that what is common knowledge in one's own circle is also common knowledge outside that circle. When in doubt about citing or not citing a source, always cite it. It is never wrong to cite your sources.

INFORMATION PRIVACY AND POLICY

Who Owns the Information?

When information is created, the question of who owns it comes up immediately. If it is posted on the Web by the author, it is possible to simply copy or download the file. Technically, the author still has the legal rights under copyright law and therefore owns the copyright to the information. The information can be used for education and research as outlined in the fair use provisions of the law. This issue becomes important when others want to access the information.

What happens if the author cedes the copyright to a publisher and that publisher sells the content to an information aggregator? Most compilers of this kind of information sell the information to others. If a company that collects information and gets exclusive rights to that information sells it to subscribers, does that mean that only those who can afford to pay for it can get it? The author has signed away the right to sell or reproduce the information. The publisher has decided to allow only the aggregator (information collector) to publish the information, and the aggregator only allows buyers to see the information. This kind of situation limits information access to those who can afford to pay for it. The increasing number of pay-per-view information aggregators could slow the speed of research to a snail's pace by blocking access to information for those who do not have the money to pay for it.

Who Has Access to the Information?

Access is a very important consideration. Most research that goes on in the world today is based on what other researchers have done in the past. The results of those previous studies and experiments are published in reports, journals, white papers, conference proceedings, and so on. If new findings are restricted in some way so that today's researchers cannot access them with relative ease and in a short period of time, how will research continue to go forward? What about information you give out when you buy a product with a credit card or order something from a catalog? Who has the right to the use of that information? Unless you give explicit instructions otherwise, the credit card companies and catalog companies can use the information you give them, or they can sell that information to others who can then contact you or learn about your shopping preferences, annual income, credit rating, and so on.

Goal: Exercise 23 will show students how easy it is to get personal information electronically. They will also find out that people's "private" information may not be as private as they think.

Description: Using the AnyWho.com website, students will look up their own names, the name of a friend or family member, or the name of someone selected by the instructor. Students will gather all the free information they can about this person. They will also find what other information is available about this person if they are willing to pay for it.

Tips for conducting the exercise: It is useful for the instructor to have a list of names that have been looked up ahead of time to ensure that there is a listing relevant to the students. For example, look up the name of the provost of the university, the director of the library, the local television news anchor, and so on. If students do not find listings for themselves, the instructor can provide a name that will provide the desired results.

This exercise addresses ACRL Standard 5.

How Does the Electronic Environment Change an Individual's Right to Privacy?

If an individual does most of his or her research, correspondence, banking, or buying and selling online, who has the right to see those transactions and under what circumstances? Hackers have been tracked down using their Internet service providers' records of transactions. This is something akin to a phone tap on the telephone of a suspect. Used for law enforcement purposes when probable cause has been shown, this situation would not trouble most people. However, what about the "cookies" that websites place on your computer when you access those sites? What do those cookies actually do? What can outsiders do with the cookies on your computer? What about the situation during which your computer is always connected to the Internet via a DSL? Can the information residing on your computer be tapped without probable cause and without a court order? Can companies track what and from whom you have bought things? Can "Big Brother" tell what sites you are visiting? Who has access to information about what you have accessed online? When you agree to make your computer a server in order to get a service (like Napster, for example), what information that resides on your computer is available for outsiders to look at?

PRIVACY ISSUES

The issue of privacy is very complex and subject to opinion and interpretation. Many people are unaware that information about them is gathered from many different electronic sources. They may not know that using a particular Internet site or tool may authorize the site owners to use the information collected in various ways. Some people do not want any information about themselves available in a public forum. Others have little or no concern in this regard. The events of September 11, 2001, and the perceived need for agencies to be able to access personal information more easily complicate the issue even further. If having specific information available to the government for reasons of national security is necessary to keep everyone safe, is it better to give up some amount of privacy?

Exercise 23

Privacy and the Internet

Go to the AnyWho.com website. Type in your own name. If there are no results for your name, use the name of someone in the business community in your area or a name provided by your instructor.

What name did you search?

How many listings were there for that name?

Select one listing. How many things can you find out about the person whose name you selected?

What were you able to find out about that individual with no cost to you?

What would you be able to find out if you were willing to pay for the information?

How much would it cost to access the public records of the person you looked up?

How do you feel about having this type and amount of information available electronically to anyone in the world?

Now think about social-networking sites like Facebook and MySpace. How many clicks does it take to get to personal information about someone who is a complete stranger to you?

Think about your earlier answers. What and how much do you want strangers to know about you?

If you apply for a high-level job and your potential employer goes to a social-networking site to gather information about you, what will he or she find there? Is there information someone else posted or tagged that might not encourage this person to hire you?

Goal: The goal of exercise 24 is to make students aware of the issues surrounding the topic of privacy and the complexity of coming to any conclusions as to where the rights of the individual stop and the needs for national security, or commerce, or other group needs begin.

Description: Have students log on to the Electronic Privacy Information Center (EPIC) website, at www.epic.org. Select one of the listed topics. Have the students explore the topic and then discuss the issue as a whole. For example, have students look at the following file at the EPIC site: www.epic.org/privacy/internet/cookies/.

Have students examine the issue raised regarding cookies individually or in small groups. Bring the group members back together and discuss the privacy issue and its problems as a class.

Tips for conducting the exercise: Assign pairs of students to explore an issue at the EPIC site, and, when the large group is brought back together, have each duo present what they learned to the rest of the group.

This exercise addresses ACRL Standard 5.

Preservation of the Human Record

Preservation is a very serious consideration in the electronic world of today. Many records that used to be kept on paper have been moved to the electronic environment. What happens to older records or writings in the electronic environment? What procedures are in place to preserve electronic documents for the historic record? For example, e-mail has replaced letters sent by U.S. mail in many instances. Only recently has anyone thought how to preserve those correspondences that might be of value to history or to law. During the Iran Contra investigations, President George H. W. Bush's administration members sought to destroy all their e-mail as part of a cover-up. The issue was taken to court only hours before the administration left office. Up to that point, no one had considered e-mail as part of the public record. Yet some very important communications took place via e-mail, and they could have been lost to history with one delete command to the computer. Fortunately, the judge who considered the case found that e-mail was part of the public record and acted in time to save those e-mails from destruction. But how were they saved? Are the original computers on which they reside stored in a big warehouse somewhere? Were the messages downloaded onto a supercomputer somewhere? What will ensure that we will be able to read those messages decades from now when the new technology of that era may look nothing like the technology of our own era or that of the Bush administration?

Many U.S. government documents are now available only in electronic format. This may decrease the amount of paper used in the production of these documents. However, this practice does raise a new difficulty. How will people who don't have computers or who don't have access to computers be able to obtain these documents? Will information access be limited to the rich or to those who have a computer available to them?

What Needs to Be Saved?

Do all e-mails need to be saved? Are all websites valuable to history? Who will decide? Where will they be kept? Who will be able to look at them? A website about what happened in the daily life of an adolescent teenager who just moved to a new city might not be of vital interest right now, but what about researchers of the future who want to look back to the beginnings of the electronic age to see how it affected people in their daily lives? Researchers today are seeking out diaries and journals of people who were among the first settlers of the western United States to get their views of what was important and meaningful and eventful in their lives. Might not researchers be interested in the same kinds of things on the new electronic frontier?

Exercise 24

Your Right to Privacy

Go to the Electronic Privacy Information Center (EPIC) website, at www.epic.org. Examine the issues listed on this site. Go to the link for Privacy in the EPIC Policy Archives. Select one topic from the *A–Z* list of privacy topics. Examine the issue as presented. Write down the important points, the pros and cons, and the concerns regarding this topic. Report back to the class what you learned.

> What is the issue?
>
> Why is it a problem?
>
> How does it infringe on the average person's right to privacy?
>
> What is being done about it?

Websites come and go at an amazing rate, many lasting only a few weeks or months. As this is the case, how will information be saved? Will there be a repository of abandoned websites where all inactive sites can be stored for future use? Is it the job of the government to provide a place where it will be saved? What about international correspondence, websites, and other electronic creations? Will there be a giant computer somewhere in which all these data can be stored? Will authors have any say over who stores their information?

How Will People Access What Is Saved?

What equipment will be used to keep access to these electronic files available? Consider the saga concerning the Lunar Orbiter Image Recovery Project. In 1965 it was decided to record the images beaming back from the lunar orbiter using AMPEX FR 900 two-inch-tape analog recorders. After the end of the Apollo program, the tapes were put into storage and the recorders were "surplussed." When interest in the lunar images revived, more than forty years later, there were no working tape drives readily available. Scientists working on the project had to find "surplussed" tape drives in order to salvage the parts needed to create a working machine that would allow the tapes to be viewed. It was only by luck that they were able to find the parts they needed to view the valuable images of the moon (www.collectspace.com/news-111408a.htm). Will everything that is happening in today's electronic environment be lost when the next new technology comes along and replaces the floppy disk, the CD, the DVD, and so on?

Who Is Responsible for Keeping, Storing, and Providing Access to Today's Information?

Will it be necessary to create a new government agency to collect, preserve, and provide access to information that is only available in electronic format? Will libraries become the repository of these new formats for information? What will become of information from other countries? Will a global mass of information be kept on the International Space Station? Will the government decide what is worth keeping and what is to be thrown away? How will those decisions be made?

It is clear that many questions about electronic information cannot yet be answered. It is very possible that valuable information will be lost now and in the future because of a lack of methods for collecting, storing, and accessing it. Some information will be saved by luck, some by law, and some by stubborn souls who will not allow information to simply disappear. At this moment, we have many more questions than we have solutions to the issues of the information age.

Note

1. *Encyclopedia of Computers and Computer History,* edited by Raúl Rojas (Chicago: Fitzroy Dearborn, 2001), 2:828.

Chapter Six

Books and Catalogs

Today's students are likely to begin a research project by searching for information on the Internet. They will use other information sources and formats only if the Internet fails them. Without a helpful introduction to the value and use of books in research, students might easily glide right by the bookshelves, assuming that the information in books is old and therefore useless. Students need to practice finding and evaluating monographic information so that they can develop a command for when and how to use books in research.

Before students can evaluate the content or begin to appreciate the organizational structure of the book, they must be able to actually find a book in the library at your institution. Some students are not familiar with the size or organizational layout of an academic library. Even though many students are adept at surfing the Web, most seem to find it difficult to use an online library catalog. This may be because many students have hidden anxiety about using library research tools and the catalog!

Catalogs help people to identify and find things. There is a catalog for almost any product or service that one can imagine. Paging through a clothing catalog or surfing a web-based catalog to find a product or service is a familiar activity for today's students, but transferring that skill to the use of the library catalog may require instruction.

WHAT *IS* A CATALOG? WHAT'S *IN* A CATALOG?

Catalogs allow us to know that an item exists by listing and describing attributes that can give us clues to its value to our research. However, as researchers, we need to obtain far greater informational detail to truly understand the value of each item that is listed within the catalog. To accurately evaluate an item from the library catalog, it is necessary to have access to its contents.

Goal: In exercise 25 students will gain an understanding of what kinds of information catalogs provide and how catalogs can differ from one another.

Description: Small groups of students will examine multiple catalogs. They will discuss several questions that will help them identify the uses and the limitations of the catalogs. Finally, students will compare the catalogs with the library catalog to identify the similarities and differences.

Exercise 25

Group Discussion: What *Is* a Catalog? What's *In* a Catalog?

Look up a dictionary definition of the word *catalog*.

> Name any catalogs that you are familiar with.
>
> Make a list of all the catalogs mentioned on a chalkboard or flip chart.
>
> What kinds of information do the catalogs offer?
>
> How are the catalogs organized?
>
> What similarities are there in the way that this information is offered?
>
> What do the catalogs have in common?
>
> What do they all do for the reader?
>
> After five minutes, record your groups' ideas on the board or flip chart, organizing them into categories as you go along: type of item, product name, classification and identification code, size, color, availability, cost.

Compare the library catalog record printouts handed out to the item records in other catalogs and answer the questions below.

> Do all types of catalogs provide similar information?
>
> What does that tell us about our library's catalog?
>
> What can we use it for?
>
> Identify and list what the catalogs do not do.
>
> Would you be able to accurately evaluate an item from a catalog, based on the catalog record?
>
> Could you try it on for size?
>
> Could you taste it?
>
> Could you be sure that the product actually matches the information needed?

Tips for conducting the exercise: Gather a wide variety of catalogs: garden, sports equipment, clothing, book club, record club, music store, museum, art gallery, and university or college catalogs. Have at least two different types of catalogs for each small group in the class. Also provide students with Internet access to your library catalog, or print several bibliographic records from your catalog for students to examine.

This exercise addresses ACRL Standard 1, Performance Indicator 2; and Standard 2, Performance Indicator 1.

FINDING BOOKS IN THE LIBRARY

The first few attempts at using a college or university library can be a difficult experience for many students. There is a reticence to embarking on the adventure when faced with both the size of the library building and the size of the collections in higher education libraries.

Goal: Students will gain an appreciation for and recognition of the importance of the Library of Congress Classification System in exercise 26.

Description: The instructor will provide each student or pair of students with an index card listing the title and author of a book available in the library. Students will search for the book without using the catalog or the library staff. They may utilize any signage available and their common sense! After ten minutes, the class regroups to discuss the results of the search. This discussion is a good lead-in to learning how to use a library catalog.

Tips for conducting the research: Check the library catalog to identify monographs that are available. On the index card for each item to be searched, list only the complete title of the book and author's name. It is best to use books with somewhat ambiguous titles so that the subject is not overly obvious.

This exercise addresses ACRL Standard 1, Performance Indicators 1 and 4.

THE BIBLIOGRAPHIC RECORD

Library catalogs include all the necessary information to describe an item, tell us if our library owns it, and if so, how we can find it. Most students are not enamored of the details of the MARC record, nor do they desire to understand the intricacy with which librarians build bibliographic records to provide individual record access to unique titles. However, the more students know about the details of the bibliographic record, the more time they will save in their hunt for appropriate research materials in the library.

Goal: Students will gain understanding of the elements included in a library catalog bibliographic record in exercise 27.

Description: Explain that library catalogs are made up of a large number of bibliographic records. Each record contains information about a unique item in the library's collection. Identify and explain the elements of the bibliographic record. After a brief introduction to parts or fields of the bibliographic record, ask students to use their own unique personal information to complete a bibliographic record about themselves, identifying and relating the elements of the format to reflect their own information.

Tips for conducting the research: Provide a complete bibliographic record that the students can use as a model for creating their own bibliographic record. Use a record for a title many students will have read in high school, such as *Catcher in the Rye*, by J. D. Salinger, or *The Color Purple*, by Alice Walker. It may be helpful to create a blank bibliographic record form based on your library's catalog software system for the students to use.

This exercise addresses ACRL Standard 1, Performance Indicator 2, and Standard 2, Performance Indicator 1.

It doesn't take long for students who are looking for research materials in any library to agree that knowing the call number of a particular item is very important. Assuming their previous experience has been in using the Dewey decimal system, the Library of Congress Classification System will seem like another enormous hurdle to jump. To a new library researcher, the Library of Congress Classification System, with its twenty broad areas of knowledge, classes, and subclasses, can sound like a college course in itself! There are several quick methods to help students learn to use the LC System, including library-created guides and handouts, locally made and proprietary online computer tutorials, and the "book truck rodeo," which is described in exercise 28.

READING LIBRARY OF CONGRESS CALL NUMBERS

It is helpful to do a quick introduction to the catalog using an online "walking tour" to familiarize students with the look and feel of the catalog system. Design

---

Exercise 26

Free-Range Searching

The index card you have been given contains basic information about a book in this library. The card lists the author's name and the complete title of the book. Your task is to use this information to find this exact book in the library and bring it back to the class, without using the catalog or any library personnel. You have ten minutes to search for and retrieve the book you have been assigned. At the end of the time period, return to the class with or without the book in hand. At that point, we will discuss the results of everyone's "free-range" search.

> How did it feel to be searching with so few clues?
>
> Did you learn or notice anything helpful about the library while you were searching?
>
> Did you see anything that could provide clues to help you to find your book?
>
> What other information do you think you need to know to have a more successful search?

---

the walking tour to cover both basic and advanced catalog search skills as time allows. Also consider using this method to provide opportunities for students to explore other features that your library catalog offers, such as limiting, scoping, and restricting searches.

Goal: In exercise 28 students will be introduced to the Library of Congress Classification System.

Description: The instructor will use a handout or website to teach students how to read the LC System numbers or call numbers. Students will then apply this knowledge to two groups of books in a "book truck rodeo," where they may earn a small prize for accuracy and speed.

Tips for conducting the exercise: For each group of three or four students, provide a book truck with one shelf of books (approximately twenty) from a wide range of LC classifications. For rodeo prizes, you might award extra-credit points or hard candies. Be sure to have a watch with a second hand or a timer available for this exercise so you can identify the winner of the rodeo.

This exercise addresses ACRL Standard 2, Performance Indicators 2 and 3.

CONTROLLED VOCABULARY AND SUBJECT HEADINGS

Today's web-savvy students often try searching the library catalog using natural language and keyword searches. The idea of using formalized subject terminology is relatively unknown to them. It takes time for them to recognize that in research there are formalized language systems such as the Library of Congress Subject Headings (LCSH) and database descriptors that help ferret out the information they need.

Goal: In exercise 29 students will learn the use of a controlled vocabulary system and improve their search results when using the library catalog.

Description: Students will search the library catalog for an assigned term or phrase, using the keyword search function. They will note the total number of items found. They will identify the LC Subject Headings in some of the records for the titles they find. They will select one or two subject headings and do a search using the subject search function. The results of the two searches will then be compared.

Tips for conducting the exercise: This exercise is best done with pairs of students or in a small-group setting. Topics we have used for this exercise include binge drinking among college students, ocean dumping, Jim Crow, the Vietnam War, World War II, nursing careers, legalization of marijuana in the United States, Samuel Clemens, and Italian cooking.

This exercise addresses ACRL Standard 1, Performance Indicator 1, and Standard 2, Performance Indicator 2.

EVALUATION

In research, each of the sources that students select must be evaluated for a variety of criteria: authorship, credibility, accuracy, reliability, currency, timeliness, scope, coverage, and relevance. Students must practice the application of evaluation criteria to each source, rather than simply using those sources that they find first or that come to hand most easily. An easy first step in learning to apply evaluation criteria is to evaluate several books on the same subject or topic and compare the results.

EVALUATING BOOKS

Convincing students that they themselves are the filters of the information that they choose to use and include in their research is no easy task. If you teach students to recognize when information is valuable for their information needs—and when it isn't—this

---

Exercise 27

Build It Yourself: Your Own Bibliographic Record

Using your knowledge of the parts and fields of a bibliographic record, use the printout provided by the instructor as a model to create a bibliographic record for yourself. Use all of the fields included in the three major parts of the record: bibliographic, location, and descriptive.

- Were you able to completely and accurately describe yourself using the bibliographic record format?

- Do you see any limitations to the format?

- Does having a bibliographic record for an item tell a researcher enough to judge the value of the work to them as a researcher?

- Does there seem to be a most important part of the record? If so, what would it be?

Exercise 28

Book Truck Rodeo!

Warm-ups

Practice putting the books on your assigned book truck in order as they would be on a library shelf. When you feel certain that the books on your truck are in the correct order, ask the instructor to check and approve your work. If necessary, practice once or twice more until you are comfortable with the concepts of the Library of Congress Classification System.

The Rodeo

Switch book trucks with another group in the class. Now you will be timed for accuracy and efficiency! Put the "new" book truck in order as accurately and as quickly as you can. Your instructor will act as timekeeper. The first group to complete the shelving accurately wins the prize!

important skill will stay with them throughout their lives.

Goal: In exercise 30 students will practice applying evaluation criteria to research materials.

Description: In small groups, students will apply evaluation criteria to several different books on the same topic and answer questions about the process. The groups will report back to the class on their findings. Contrasts, similarities, and comparisons will be observed.

Tips for conducting the exercise: For each group of students, gather three books on a topic. Each group should have a different topic to better illustrate that evaluation criteria can change based on the material. Some suggestions for topics are nuclear energy, climate change, and drug abuse. One of the books could be "perfect" (based on the criteria) for the group's assigned topic, one could be outdated, and one could be from an unidentifiable source. This exercise is best done by pairs of students or small groups.

This exercise addresses ACRL Standard 3, Performance Indicator 2.

ANNOTATED BIBLIOGRAPHY OF BOOKS

Providing students with a variety of hands-on opportunities to explore the library's catalog allows them to become effective searchers able to find and locate books in the library. Understanding that finding the right books need not be a "needle in a haystack" situation goes a long way to building research confidence in college students. Writing a summary of a book and offering evaluative information to other readers is another way to help students learn how to select quality information.

Goal: In exercise 31 students will gain practice in citation style, annotating, and briefly evaluating books as they relate to a specific information need.

Description: The instructor provides instructions and a guide for students to follow. Students will use the library catalog to find five books on a preapproved topic. Students will write citations, annotations, and brief evaluative comments about each of the books selected.

Tips for conducting the exercise: Show students how to identify and review the parts of a book used for annotating: table of contents, index, preface or introduction, and book arrangement. Supply a sample citation, an example annotation, and an evaluative criteria chart.

This exercise addresses ACRL Standard 1, Performance Indicators 1, 3, and 4; Standard 2, Performance Indicators 1, 2, 3, 4, and 5; Standard 3, Performance Indicators 1 and 2; Standard 4, Performance Indicators 2 and 3; and Standard 5, Performance Indicators 1 and 3.

Exercise 29

Using Keywords to Identify Subject Headings

You will receive an index card with a word or phrase on it. Search the library catalog for the topic on the index card by using the keyword or "word search" function.

How many items did you find listed?

Browse through the titles. Are all the titles listed relevant to your topic?

Go to the full bibliographic record for two or three titles from the list. Find the "Subject" field in the bibliographic record for each item and examine the Library of Congress Subject Headings (LCSH) listed. Find and record all of the LCSH for each book. Be thorough.

Which subject heading do you think best describes the topic on your index card? You may feel that there is more than one; if so, select more than one.

Use the subject search in the library catalog and type in one of the LCSH you selected above. How many subjects were found?

Does the catalog provide any "Related Subjects"? If so, list one or two.

In the space below, note one or two subdivisions of your LCSH. For example, "The main LCSH is 'Electronic Commerce,' but in searching for that subject heading, I also see 'Electronic Commerce—Asia' and 'Electronic Commerce—Economic Aspects.'"

How many items were found under the main LCSH you typed in? Look at the titles retrieved. Are the titles listed relevant to your topic?

Overall, which search method ("Word Search" or "Subject" search) produced more focused, effective results?

Why do you think this was the case? Be able to explain.

Evaluating Books for Value

You have been given three books to evaluate. They are all about the same topic, but there is no guarantee that all three are quality sources of information. Your job is to use the evaluative criteria listed below and to take notes on how each source answers the evaluation criteria. In fifteen or twenty minutes, your group will report back to the class with your findings on the three information sources.

First—Review the Bibliographic Information

Author(s): What is their authority or credibility? Do they have the expertise to say or write what they did? What is their educational background? What is their career experience?

Date of Publication: When was the source published? Is the book a recent publication or is the information out-of-date for the topic?

Edition or Revision: Is this book a first edition? If it is a second or multiple-edition copy, can you tell how it is different from earlier editions?

Publisher: Who is the publisher? Is it a university press? Do you recognize the publisher?

Next—Do a Content Analysis

Purpose: Why was this written? What is the intent of the author? Who is the intended audience? Who is the author trying to inform or influence?

Relevance: Is the material appropriate and useful for your research? Does it answer all or part of your research question? Can it be used for background or to focus on a specific area?

Scope and Coverage of Material: Can you tell if the author intends to provide comprehensive coverage of a subject or topic? What are the limitations of the information? What time period is covered? Where was it published? Does geographical area impact the informational content?

Objectivity: Do you see any evidence of bias, propaganda, or a strong persuasive argument? Is the material viewed from more than one point of view? Does it contain substantiated fact?

Writing Quality: Is it clear to you what the author intends to share and express? Is there evidence of clear organization and writing? Has it been well researched? Are there any obvious pieces of information missing?

Writing an Annotated Bibliography of Books

This exercise contains many research skills that you will need to be an effective researcher in college: finding books, citing sources, summarizing information, and evaluating materials for your research needs. A bibliography is a list of sources that were used as resource material for the paper or project at hand. For this exercise,

Search the library catalog for your topic.

Find five books on your topic and retrieve them.

Examine the books you found and determine whether or not they are appropriate for your topic.

If they are not appropriate, go back to the library catalog until you have identified five appropriate books.

Print out the full bibliographic record from the catalog for each of the five books.

Next, photocopy the title page of each of the books.

On a separate piece of paper, following the example provided below, type the citation for each book, providing all relevant information. The citation should follow this format:

Last name of author, First name. *The Title of the Book* [this is capitalized and put in italics]: *The Subtitle* [this is also included, capitalized, and put in italics]. City: Publisher, Year.

Beneath each citation, using your own words, type an annotation. An annotation is a brief descriptive and evaluative note that provides enough information about the book so a person can decide whether or not to consult the book.

To write an annotation, you will comment, in paragraph form, on the following elements:

Content—What's the book about? Is it relevant to your research?

Purpose—What's it for? Why was this book written?

Methods used to collect data—Where did the information come from?

Usefulness—What does it do for your research?

Reliability—Is the information accurate?

Authority—Is it written by someone who has the expertise to author the information?

Currency—Is it new? Is it up-to-date for the topic?

Scope/Coverage/Limitations—What does it cover? What does the author state that he or she will cover? What doesn't the book provide that would be helpful?

Arrangement—How is the book organized? Are there any special "added-value" features?

Ease of use—Can a nonspecialist use this book? What reading level is the book?

Here is a sample citation and annotation to get you started:

List, Carla J. *Information Research*. 2nd ed. Dubuque, IA.: Kendall/Hunt, 2002. In this book, Carla J. List, an award-winning teacher and librarian, defines and describes information and provides step-by-step instruction on doing research. In seven chapters, she covers the organization of information, information technology, and the presentation, analysis, evaluation, and citation of information. A bibliography, glossary, and index are included. This book is aimed at the college-level student and is useful to the inexperienced researcher.

SUBJECT-SPECIFIC INFORMATION LITERACY INSTRUCTION

Contributed by Peter J. Larsen

This section describes a general library session dealing with beginning instruction in basic library skills, filtered through the lens of a specific subject—in this case, engineering. The exercises can be adapted to accommodate any subject.

The Introductory Engineering course at the University of Rhode Island provides a basic introduction to the university, the engineering programs, basic academic skills necessary for the engineering student (including information literacy), and first-year contact with engineering professors. Approximately three hundred students take the course in the fall semester.

The library instruction session is delivered in lecture format, focusing on general information about library services, engineering library needs, ethical use of information in an engineering context, and background on library tools. The lecture is followed by a seventy-five-minute lab session, where the students observe demonstrations of catalog and database searching and participate in hands-on, in-class practice. To draw the student's attention to engineering elements, engineering-specific topics are used in learning to search both the online catalog and the Compendex (an engineering database) index. The techniques taught are very general—although the examples are engineering-based, the skills are entirely transferable to other search topics.

Engineering Library Assignment

This library assignment, though focused on engineering, can be adapted for use with any topic.

Goal: In exercise 32, students will gain basic fluency with the online catalog and a subject-specific index. They will also be exposed to the basic services of the library.

Description: The seventy-five-minute lab session includes these elements:

- an online catalog demonstration (ten minutes)
- using the catalog to answer questions (fifteen minutes)
- a short Compendex demonstration (fifteen minutes)
- using the index to answer questions (twenty minutes)
- completion of a worksheet

The assignment is graded on a scale of one to ten (roughly one point off for each three wrong answers) and returned to the faculty teaching the course for inclusion in the final grade.

Tips for conducting the exercise: Work with the course instructor to make the assessment of the practice worksheet part of the course grade. This is essential, especially in the sciences, where students are often highly focused on short-term goals to the exclusion of long-term skill acquisition.

The worksheet must be adapted to be institution-specific, but the basic outline should work in any setting.

Focus on finding and using discipline-specific tools (e.g., handbooks for engineers and scientists).

Similarly, use local-faculty-written articles as examples, because this increases the students' interest. The hints and notes in the questions help students find the correct answer. Questions can be easily modified and removed or added to fit shorter or longer session times.

This exercise addresses ACRL "Information Literacy Standards for Science and Engineering/Technology" (www.ala.org/ala/mgrps/divs/acrl/standards/infolitsci tech.cfm) Standard 2, Performance Indicators 1, 2, and 3. The complete session, as taught, adds Standard 1, Performance Indicators 2 and 3, and Standard 5, Performance Indicator 1.

Subject-Specific Library Skills

A. Finding Books

1. Using the online catalog, find the book [insert title of an engineering book from your library]. Answer the following questions:

   Which of the subject headings will be most useful to you to find more information on this topic?

   What is the call number?

   Where will you find it in the library?

   When was the book published?

   Because [insert the book's topic] technology is rapidly developing, current information is a must. Do you think this book is recent enough for your research?

   The publisher is [insert publisher's name], a commercial publisher. Based on what the publisher has to say about itself at its website [insert publisher's URL], do you believe that this publisher will provide good information? Why or why not?

2. Using the online catalog again, find a book with some basic information (simple explanations and stress values) for a project using concrete.

   What search did you use? (a) Project using concrete; (b) Project concrete; (c) Concrete handbook; (d) Basic concrete

   How many items did you find?

   What is the title of the most recent book on the list?

   What is the call number?

   Where in the library will you find this book?

   Can you check it out, or do you have to use it in the library?

B. Finding Articles

1. Using Compendex, look for an article using the search "traffic and rhode island" (ignore the quotes) and limit it to journal articles.

   An article in the list (it's about Newport) was written by someone at the University of Rhode Island. Who?

   What is the serial title?

   When was the article published?

   Is the article available at [insert name of your institution]? (circle all that apply) Yes, in paper / Yes, electronically / No

   Looking at the abstract, list two of the factors associated with renewal causing "negative attitudes" in the residents.

2. You've overheard Professor Swaszek talking about GPS with a colleague. You want to impress him, so you decide to use your database skills to find something on the topic so you can ask him about his publications. See if you can find an article written by Professor Swaszek on GPS using Compendex. Note: a correct search will find more than one article; because you want to be current, pick the most recent one.

   What is the article title?

   What is the serial title?

(cont.)

What are the volume, issue, and year?

Is the article available at [insert name of your institution]? (circle all that apply)
Yes, in paper / Yes, electronically / No

3. You have the following citation: Wilson, Simon, et al. "Optical Guidance Systems for Industrial Robots." *Journal of Robotic Systems* 9.3 (1992): 275–290. (Note: before trying this, ask yourself—what tool tells you what materials are available in the library?)

Is it available at [insert name of your institution]?

If so, what is the call number?

Where in the library would you find it?

Which years are available?

Given the speed of technological development, would this periodical be useful to you for a project today?

C. Using the Library

1. Where can you access most electronic resources?

    a. Only on campus

    b. Only in the dorms

    c. From anywhere I can find a web-ready computer

    d. Only in the library

2. When you are stuck in your research, who is your pal at the library?

    a. Circulation librarians

    b. Reference librarians

    c. Google

    d. I will just ask my professor

3. You are doing a semester-long senior project, and you find an article in an index that is perfect for your research. Unfortunately, your institution doesn't have it. What do you do?

    a. Forget about it; something else will come along.

    b. Make an interlibrary loan request, because I can wait two to three weeks.

    c. Ask my professor if he or she has a copy.

    d. Look for the article on the Web.

Chapter Seven

Periodicals and Databases

Teaching students how to work with periodical information is a major part of any program for information literacy. Within the context of a formal course in information literacy, it is often the case that more time will be spent on periodical information—what a periodical is, what types of periodicals exist, how to identify periodical articles on a topic, how indexing and abstracting databases work, how to locate periodicals once a citation is found—than on any other single topic. Using periodicals as sources of information seems to be most preferred by students and is often required by their instructors. The exercises in this chapter provide a number of examples that have proved effective in exploring the multifaceted topic of periodical research, but, of course, there are many other similar exercises available, and even more yet to be created.

USING PERIODICALS

After becoming comfortable with using library catalogs to identify and locate books, students are now ready to face the more complicated task of researching their topic using periodical articles.

Before searching for articles in indexes and indexing and abstracting databases, it is helpful to establish clearly what a periodical is. The *International Encyclopedia of Information and Library Science* defines a periodical as "a publication appearing at regular and fixed intervals of time under a distinctive title. . . . Its contents are usually some mixture of articles, reviews, stories or other writings by several contributors."[1] Periodicals can be published daily, weekly, monthly, quarterly, and so on.

It is helpful to remind students why periodicals are useful sources when doing research. Periodicals are important sources because they are published more frequently than books, they are more accessible, and they appear in a more finished form than other sources in the information cycle such as conference papers, patents, or working papers shared between colleagues. In general, periodicals tend to be the place where new knowledge is first revealed. Periodicals usually contain the most current information on a topic. Currency is especially important for science and social sciences research topics.

To really understand what periodicals are and how they differ from one another requires an even closer look, or an understanding of the taxonomy of periodicals. In our taxonomy, we divide periodicals into three major categories:

- popular magazines and newspapers
- professional, trade, and industry or special-interest periodicals
- scholarly, academic, peer-reviewed, or refereed journals

The quality and characteristics of the information found in each type of periodical vary. The criteria below will help students understand the characteristics of each type and how to distinguish between them.

The material in figure 7.1 should be considered broad guidelines and should not be taken as absolute rules.

THE TAXONOMY OF PERIODICALS

After studying the types of periodicals (as shown in figure 7.1), students should explore periodicals themselves, with an eye toward identification of the critical differences among different types of publications.

Goal: In exercise 33 students will familiarize themselves with different types of periodicals that they will encounter during their research. This exercise also reinforces the critical thinking emphasized throughout this book.

Description: Students will work in teams of two or three. The instructor will pass out the worksheet to each group along with three periodical titles, all related to the same general topic. One of the three should be from each category of periodical as defined above. Students will closely examine each periodical and decide which of the three categories it falls under and why. After students have completed the exercise, the groups will introduce their periodicals to the rest of the class, explaining the characteristics of each.

In figure 7.2 are some examples of groups of periodicals that have been used in this exercise.

Tips for conducting the exercise: You may wish to bring two copies of each of the three publications. This way, more than one student in each group can

examine the same periodical at the same time. This in-class exercise can easily be adapted as a take-home assignment. This exercise also works well when you give the students the publications and allow them to create their own chart, identifying attributes that allow the identification of specific types of publications.

This exercise addresses ACRL Standard 1, Performance Indicator 2, and Standard 3, Performance Indicators 2 and 6.

POPULAR VERSUS SCHOLARLY PUBLICATIONS

Here is another way of allowing students to discover the differences between popular and scholarly publications.

Goal: In exercise 34 students will improve database-searching skills and be able to determine the differences and uses of both popular and scholarly periodical articles, with particular focus on authority, audience, and purpose.

Description: Students will be given an article from a newspaper or magazine that reports or highlights a recent research study. Topics that work well for this exercise include coffee and health, chocolate and health, and wine and health. The pair of articles cited below address resveratrol and the possible positive effects of drinking red wine on a long life!

Exercise 33

Types of Periodicals— Can You Tell Them Apart?

Work in pairs or threes. Each group will be given three periodicals. Take a few minutes to look carefully at each periodical. As a group, discuss the characteristics of each. Using the criteria presented in the "Taxonomy of Periodicals" in figure 7.1, please decide in which category (popular magazines; professional, trade, and industry or special-interest periodicals; or scholarly, academic, peer-reviewed, or refereed journals) each of your periodicals best fits. Then, on a sheet of paper with your names at the top, write the titles of each of your periodicals, what type of periodical you think each is, and why you came to this conclusion, providing specific evidence from the periodicals themselves. Be prepared to introduce each of your periodicals to the class and to explain why it is a good representative of its category.

"Did You Hear about That Study?"
Team Exercise for Understanding Periodical Types

Take a few minutes to look carefully at the two articles you have found about the research study. Discuss the differences between them. Fill in your observations in the grid below.

CRITERIA	PERIODICAL A NAME: _____	PERIODICAL B NAME: _____
Intended audience (Who would be likely to read this and why? What is the purpose of the periodical?)		
Authors (Can you find the expertise or credentials of the authors?)		
Purpose (Is it research, general news, or entertainment?)		
Reliability/accuracy (What evidence of either can you identify?)		
Article length (Estimate words, columns, pages.)		
Reading level (Simple language or jargon/ lingo? How difficult?)		
Graphics (How many? What type?)		
Footnotes (Are sources cited at the end of articles?)		

Wrap up! Which article is more useful? How? Why?

University of Rhode Island Libraries, Library 120 Instructor Group, 8/09

Figure 7.1

TAXONOMY OF PERIODICALS

LOOK AT THE . . .	POPULAR MAGAZINES AND NEWSPAPERS	PROFESSIONAL, TRADE, AND INDUSTRY OR SPECIAL-INTEREST PERIODICALS	SCHOLARLY, ACADEMIC, PEER-REVIEWED, OR REFEREED JOURNALS
Citation			
Title	May have *magazine* or popular words in the title (e.g., *BusinessWoman, Mother Jones, People Weekly*)	Sometimes has *news* in the title (e.g., *Metal Construction News, AAUP News*). Titles tend to be short and practical (e.g., *Beverage World, Hotel Business*)	May have *bulletin, journal,* or *review* in the title (e.g., *Bulletin of Atomic Scientists, Journal of Soil and Water Conservation, International Review of Hydrobiology*)
Frequency of publication	Issued frequently: weekly, biweekly, or monthly	Issued frequently: weekly, biweekly, or monthly	Issued less frequently: monthly, quarterly, or semiannually
Authors of articles	Often one author. Staff-written or written by freelance authors or guest contributors	Often one author. Staff-written or written by freelance authors, guest contributors, or professionals in the field	Frequently multiple coauthors. Scholars and researchers in the field, discipline, or specialty. Authors with university affiliations or professional titles
Article length	Articles usually short	Articles usually short	Longer articles (more than three pages)
Article titles	Popular or catchy article titles	Straightforward article titles, sometimes popular and catchy	Titles related to research question or results; often long, not catchy
Whole Periodical			
Paper, illustrations, layout	Eye-catching covers, glossy paper, photos, illustrations, cartoons, sidebars	Eye-catching covers, glossy paper, photos, illustrations, cartoons, sidebars	Plain covers, usually plain matte paper; mostly text inside, with tables, figures, charts, graphs; little or no color or illustrations

LOOK AT THE . . .	POPULAR MAGAZINES AND NEWSPAPERS	PROFESSIONAL, TRADE, AND INDUSTRY OR SPECIAL-INTEREST PERIODICALS	SCHOLARLY, ACADEMIC, PEER-REVIEWED, OR REFEREED JOURNALS
Advertising	Many ads for general-consumer products and services	Many ads for products and services related to a particular profession, trade, or industry	Few or no ads; if any, tend to be for other journals or specific services or products
Tone	Slick, glossy, attractive	Slick, glossy, attractive	Serious, unembellished
Audience	Educated but nonexpert readers; uses simple language in order to meet minimum education levels	Practitioners of a particular profession, members of a trade, or workers in an industry; language appropriate for an educated readership; assumes a certain level of specialized knowledge	Scholars and researchers in the field, discipline, or specialty; language contains terminology and jargon of the discipline; reader is assumed to have a scholarly background
Purpose	Designed to entertain or persuade readers with a variety of general interest topics in broad subject fields; also geared to sell products and services through advertising	Examines problems or concerns in a particular profession or industry; provides specialized information to a wide, interested audience	To inform, report, or make available original research or experimentation in a specific field or discipline to the rest of the scholarly world; where "new knowledge" is reported
Availability	Likely to be found on a newsstand or in a magazine store	Rarely found on a newsstand or in a magazine store; requires subscription or library access	With some exceptions, not found on a newsstand or in a magazine store; requires subscription or library access

Articles

Abstracts	Articles do not have an abstract at the beginning	Articles do not have an abstract at the beginning	Articles usually have an abstract at the beginning that summarizes the findings of the article

(cont.)

Figure 7.1 (cont.)

LOOK AT THE . . .	POPULAR MAGAZINES AND NEWSPAPERS	PROFESSIONAL, TRADE, AND INDUSTRY OR SPECIAL-INTEREST PERIODICALS	SCHOLARLY, ACADEMIC, PEER-REVIEWED, OR REFEREED JOURNALS
References	Sources are not cited; no references or bibliography at end of articles	Sources are not cited; no references or bibliography at end of articles	Scholarly references in the form of bibliographies, reference lists, and footnotes appear with each article
Examples	*Glamour, People Weekly, Reader's Digest, Newsweek*	*Beverage World, Restaurant News, Advertising Age*	*Science, JAMA: Journal of the American Medical Association, Academy of Management Journal, Psychological Bulletin*

- Assign pairs of students to work together.
- Give each pair of students the citation, or the actual article, for a newspaper or magazine article that highlights the research done for a study on a particular societal or health issue of contemporary interest.
- Instruct students to search the article for clues about what original research was done prior to the newspaper's or magazine article's report, and then to use those clues to construct a search statement that will find the article that reports the research study. Search statements generally include author name and other significant keywords.
- Students will then compare the elements of the two articles, looking for qualities that will distinguish the general from the scholarly.

Tips for conducting the exercise: Below is one pair of articles that will work for this exercise.

Article A: Tipp, David. "So What's the Scoop on That Stuff in Red Wine That's Supposed to Let You Live Forever?" *Fortune* 155.2 (05 Feb. 2007): 68–80. Academic Search Complete. EBSCO. University of Rhode Island Libraries, Kingston, RI. Aug. 31, 2009 http://0-search.ebscohost.com.helin.uri.edu/login.aspx?direct=true&db=a9h&AN=23783628&site=ehost-live.

Article B: Baur, Joseph A., et al. "Resveratrol Improves Health and Survival of Mice on a High-Calorie Diet." *Nature* 444.7117 (16 Nov. 2006): 337–342. Academic Search Complete. EBSCO. University of Rhode Island Libraries, Kingston, RI. Aug. 31, 2009 http://0-search.ebscohost.com.helin.uri.edu/login.aspx?direct=true&db=a9h&AN=23097590&site=ehost-live.

To wrap up the exercise, ask students, "What's the point?" Lead a discussion where students will decide which of the articles is more useful in a college-level project or paper. Ask students, "How is it useful?" "Why is it useful?"

This exercise addresses ACRL Standard 1, Performance Indicator 2, and Standard 3, Performance Indicators 2 and 6.

ACCESS TOOLS

Once students understand the different types of periodicals that exist and the unique characteristics of each, they are ready to learn how to use an access tool to systematically identify periodical articles about a topic.

Today's students are very familiar with the idea of typing words into a computer when using an Internet search engine or directory such as Google or Yahoo! and having search results magically appear before their eyes. We feel that students should be taken deeper into how access tools of any kind work. Instead of starting with online periodical indexes, which seem almost as magic as a web search, it helps to begin with the basics. Have students create a simple access tool to search for items in a collection.

CREATING AN ACCESS TOOL

Understanding access tools will help students search a collection for specific items. By creating their own access tool, students will think about how it works and what kinds of capabilities are necessary to allow others

to use it successfully. This should help them to use commercially produced access tools.

Goal: In exercise 35 students will gain a basic foundation of what indexing is. After building their own access tool, periodical indexes will make more sense to them, both print indexes and online indexing and abstracting databases.

Description: Students will work in teams of two or three. The instructor will give each group an index card with an imaginary collection written on it. Students are to assume that their collection has twenty-five items. They will identify common characteristics of the items in the collection and select the three they feel are most important (for example, author, title, subject). These will become their access points. They will then list each item and the specific individual characteristics of each, which will enable them to perform a simple search of the collection.

Tips for conducting the exercise: This exercise can also be used individually as a take-home assignment, in which case the instructor may wish to suggest that students use a computer software program such as Microsoft Word, Microsoft Excel, or Microsoft Access to create the graphical representation of their collection.

Collections that have been used for this exercise include a collection of souvenirs; a collection of recipes; a collection of musical sound recordings; contact information for members of an organization,

Figure 7.2

EXAMPLES OF PERIODICAL GROUPINGS FOR EXERCISE 33

POPULAR MAGAZINES	PROFESSIONAL, TRADE, AND INDUSTRY OR SPECIAL-INTEREST PERIODICALS	SCHOLARLY, ACADEMIC, PEER-REVIEWED, OR REFEREED JOURNALS
Sports Illustrated	Coach and Athletic Director	Research Quarterly for Exercise and Sport
BusinessWeek	Adweek	Journal of Marketing Research
Rolling Stone	Billboard	American Music
Prevention	Drug Store News	Journal of the American Pharmaceutical Association
American Gardener	American Nurseryman	Journal of the American Society for Horticultural Science

association, or team; the clothes in a closet; and the items in a refrigerator.

This exercise addresses ACRL Standard 1, Performance Indicator 2; Standard 2, Performance Indicators 2 and 5; and Standard 3, Performance Indicators 3 and 6.

PRINT INDEXES

Although many libraries have discarded their print indexes, they still exist. Students benefit from using the paper indexes in that they learn to read and understand the citations in the index and they learn that not all indexes are available in online format. In addition, once they have used a print index, the improvements in usability and the relative ease of access to full-text articles in online indexes is strikingly clear.

Goal: In exercise 36 students will gain an understanding of what an index is. Students will also gain appreciation of the time it takes to search print indexes and learn the difference between a general index and subject-specific indexes. Finally, they will learn that it

Exercise 35

Access Tools for Fun and Profit

Carla J. List, retired librarian and teacher of information research, writes in the second edition of her book *Information Research,* "A tool is something you use to help you accomplish a task. In the case of information research, an access tool is an information source that helps you by leading you to information. It may provide the actual material that you'll read or view, or it may only give you enough information to find that material."[2]

To create an access tool, you must investigate the material in a collection and then explain, create, and devise systems you could use to organize the collection.

For this assignment, your team of two or three people will be given an index card with a type of collection written on it. You are to assume that there are twenty-five items in your collection, which you must organize (for example, recipes, music recordings, contact information for twenty-five people, and so on).

Make a list of the twenty-five specific items in your collection. Use your imagination!

Describe your collection by listing a number of important characteristics the items in the collection all have, such as age, size, shape, color, place of origin, cultural importance, genre or type, location, and so on.

Create a table listing each item in your collection and each item's three most important characteristics. Below is an example for a collection of jewelry with six items. On a separate sheet of paper, give an example of a search you could do in your collection, using two of your access points. For example, using the collection below, you could search for "expensive and ring." Which items would appear in your "results list"?

JEWELRY PIECE (ITEM)	VALUE	MATERIAL	TYPE
Gold chain, 22k	Expensive	Gold	Necklace
Lorus watch	Cheap	Stainless steel	Watch
Swatch watch	Cheap	Plastic	Watch
Gold ring from India, 22k	Expensive	Gold	Ring
Silver bangle	Cheap	Sterling silver	Bracelet
Sapphire ring	Expensive	Sterling silver	Ring

is still sometimes necessary to use print indexes to gain access to older material.

Description: Students work with the *Readers' Guide to Periodical Literature* and two subject-specific indexes from H. W. Wilson. They complete a worksheet in class or at home that guides them through using these research tools.

Tips for conducting the exercise: If possible, make each student's worksheet slightly different (such as requiring an article from a different year) to avoid the entire class needing to work with the same print volume.

This exercise addresses ACRL Standard 1, Performance Indicator 2.

GENERAL PERIODICALS DATABASES

After introducing students to print indexes, an appropriate next step is to show them the library's general periodicals database, for example ProQuest's Research Library, EBSCO's Academic Search Premier, or Gale's Expanded Academic Index.

We often use exercise 16—"Information and Time," found in chapter 4 of this book—to give students practice in using an online database. This exercise also serves to reinforce the taxonomy of periodicals.

To supplement any exercise, instructors can assign students the task of finding several articles in the general database on their research topic. (This is similar to exercise 39.)

CREATING DATABASE SEARCH STATEMENTS

After students have gotten their feet wet with the library's general-purpose online indexing and abstracting database, they will need practice turning their research question into a search statement that databases can understand. Many students will be used to tools on the World Wide Web, such as Ask.com, where they can type in a complete question and get acceptable search results. Although some library databases are incorporating such "natural language" searches, it is still standard practice when searching indexing and abstracting databases to use Boolean logic. Being able to take a research question, identify its core concepts, think of alternate search terms, and structure a Boolean search from these elements is essential to students' research success. Without this skill, students

---

Exercise 36

Using Print Indexes

In this exercise, you will be working with three periodical indexes in print format: the *Readers' Guide to Periodical Literature,* the *Humanities Index,* and the *Social Sciences Index.* These indexes are published by H. W. Wilson, which has been producing them under one title or another since the early 1900s.

This worksheet will guide you through a few searches in these indexes. The goal of the exercise is to familiarize you with how print indexes work. This will also help you understand what goes on "behind the screen" when you search an online periodical database.

> Using the *Readers' Guide to Periodical Literature,* find an article published in [year] having to do with school violence. Write the citation for the article.
>
> Use the library's catalog to find out if the library has this issue of the periodical. Indicate whether or not the library has the issue, and, if it does, write the information necessary to locate the article.
>
> Is this article from a scholarly journal or a popular magazine?
>
> Find an article published in [year] having to do with school violence using the *Social Sciences Index.* Write the citation for the article.
>
> Which libraries in [name of your consortium] could supply this article? Name the libraries.
>
> Is this article from a scholarly journal or a popular magazine?
>
> Find an article by N. Turner about the painter Paul Cézanne, using the *Humanities Index.* Write the citation for the article.
>
> Is it possible to find this article in [name of your library]? Indicate where it would be located. Be specific.
>
> Which of the indexes above is the best for finding articles published about market research?
>
> What index would you use to find scholarly articles on philosophy?
>
> In what index would you look to find a news article about Ronald Reagan being elected president of the United States in 1980?

WHAT IS A DATABASE?

Contributed by Kate Cheromcha

In exercise 5 we had students discuss what they needed to know and where they would look for reliable information with regard to buying a car. If all that information was gathered together in one place, as in a database, it would be much easier to use. In exercise 37, students will create just such a database.

To introduce students to the concept of a database—a collection of information that has been deliberately designed for organized searching—this lesson compares the experience of searching for a suitable car in a commercial database to the experience of searching for a suitable article in a licensed, general database.

Goal: The purpose of exercise 37 is to introduce the concepts of searching—limiting, restricting, broadening, narrowing, choosing search terms, using specialized vocabulary—and how to use the database's features to improve search results.

Description: Using autotrader.com and/or cars.com, provide the one piece of information required to get started—your zip code—and ask the students to locate a car for you to purchase.

Tips for conducting the exercise: Wait for students to ask questions: "What make and model? Is a truck OK? What about a van? How much do I want to spend? What year? How far am I willing to travel to get it? How many miles? What options?" Have a student record criteria (make, model, options) on a whiteboard. Depending upon time available you can modify the exercise as follows:

- Everyone uses the same database.
- Students work in pairs or solo.
- Pairs can use the same database or each pair uses both databases.
- Divide the class in two and direct each half to search for a car—one half uses cars.com; the other uses autotrader.com.

This exercise addresses ACRL Standard 1, Performance Indicator 1; Standard 2, Performance Indicators 3, 4, and 5; Standard 3, Performance Indicators 3, 4, and 7; and Standard 4, Performance Indicators 1, 2, and 3.

Professor C. Needs a Car

Part 1

Using autotrader.com and/or cars.com, and [insert local zip code], find a car for sale—any car—for Professor C.

> How many cars did you find?
>
> How could this search be narrowed down?
>
> Record the criteria (keywords) in one column on the whiteboard while you continue searching. Try the search again, adding one criterion at a time.
>
> Did you do a search so specific that it did not find any cars?
>
> If so, prioritize the criteria by numbering items on the whiteboard list. What is most important? What is least important?
>
> Start searching from the beginning, adding criteria in priority order, one at a time. What is the smallest number of cars you would consider looking at? What is the largest number of cars you would consider looking at?
>
> What should I do before buying one of these cars and why?

Part 2

Now that we have a car to drive, let's switch gears to an academic setting. The skill set that allows you to find a car in a commercial database transfers easily to the search for articles in a periodical database. Consider some academic questions related to cars or the auto industry.

> Should teenagers be allowed to drive?
>
> Do teenagers have the "brains" to handle driving?

To best answer these academic questions, you will need good-quality, relevant information from a credible source. To find that information,

1. Use a general periodical database.
2. Determine what keywords are appropriate.
3. Write your terms and synonyms on the whiteboard.

For example:

teenager	driving	brain
teenage	driver	mind
adolescent	driv* (truncation)	mental development
+ male		brain development
		thinking/thought
		decision-making skill*

Do you see any parallels between the two databases (yours and the publisher's) and the searching experiences? Compare the databases using this handout.

(cont.)

Exercise 37 (cont.)

	AUTOTRADER.COM	**ACADEMIC SEARCH PREMIER**
Product/commodity provided	Cars, vans, trucks—transportation	Articles, book reviews, editorials—information
Purpose—why was this database created?	To allow me to find a vehicle, for buying/selling vehicles	To allow me to find information
Who pays for it? Really?	Sellers of cars, advertisers	Subscription fees, paid by university, library, subscribers; part of tuition/taxes
Who can use this database? Anyone? Anytime? Anywhere?	Anytime I want to search for a car—available 24/7.	Limited—24/7 available but only to library users, cardholders, password protected.

Think about your research need: what different ways can I search for information on it?

How can I narrow my search?	Specify: car make/model, mileage, cost, year—description	More specific search terms; identify narrow aspects of broad topic
How can I broaden my search?	Change some/all of above	Broader terms

Change boundaries around my searches to improve the results:

How can I limit my search?	Specify geographic search area; new versus used car	Specify document type, full-text only, dates
How can I expand my search?	Remove/change some of above	Remove/change some of above

Share your "best find" with the class.

will get poor results when they search library databases, and their research will not be effective.

Goal: In exercise 38 students will learn to create search statements that a database will understand.

Description: Students will work in teams of two or three. Each group will be given an index card with a research question on it. They will identify the key concepts in the question and brainstorm possible synonyms or alternate ways of phrasing each concept. Finally, they will create a Boolean search statement that will

effectively find results that address their research question. The instructor will call on as many groups as possible to have them read their research question aloud and explain their process to the class. Meanwhile, the instructor will write their words and statement on the board, with the rest of the class giving input about other synonyms or ways to phrase the search.

Tips for conducting the exercise: It is helpful if the instructor begins the class with a refresher on the Boolean operators AND, OR, and NOT. A solid understanding of Boolean searching should be enough to enable students to create effective search statements on any topic.

This exercise can easily be followed up with an exercise in searching subject-specific databases. For example, students who created a search statement in the area of literature could run their search statement through the MLA Bibliography. This would give them familiarity with the database and also allow them to test the effectiveness of the search statement they created.

Here are three examples of research questions in the humanities, the social sciences, and science that have been used for this exercise.

Humanities. Frederick Law Olmstead (1822–1903) was a landscape architect who designed a number of public parks, including Central Park in New York City. Olmstead was well known for his political opinions; for example, he was a vocal opponent of slavery. He was also the founder of the *Nation*, the oldest continuously published American periodical in existence and still one of the leading liberal magazines of its kind. How were Olmstead's political views reflected in his designs of public space?

Social Sciences. There are many arguments for and against the legalization of illicit drugs. One argument for legalization states that overall demand for illegal drugs would go down if drugs were legalized because the allure of doing something forbidden would disappear. Find both support for and criticism of this viewpoint.

Science. With the ongoing destruction of rain forests and other habitats, the number of plant and animal species facing extinction continues to grow. What are the implications of this loss of biodiversity on the development of new pharmaceutical drugs?

This exercise addresses ACRL Standard 1, Performance Indicator 1, and Standard 2, Performance Indicators 2, 3, and 4.

SUBJECT-SPECIFIC PERIODICALS DATABASES

A major project on subject-specific indexing and abstracting databases, the Team Database Discovery Project (exercise 39) is used in the context of a three-

---

Exercise 38

Creating Effective Search Statements

You will receive an index card with a research question on it. Working as a group, please:

Pick out the key concepts in your research question.

If appropriate, list some synonyms or alternate ways of phrasing each of your key concepts. Use the form below.

KEY CONCEPT	SYNONYMS OR ALTERNATE WAYS OF PHRASING

Structure a search statement that you could use for researching this topic in a database. Use Boolean operators (AND, OR, NOT) when appropriate.

Be prepared to share your research question, key concepts and synonyms, and search statement with the class.

credit course in which it alone accounts for 10 percent of each student's grade.

There are many active learning methods by which students can become familiar with the many indexing and abstracting databases available in libraries. For example, an exercise similar to exercise 36 could be used to guide students step-by-step through a number of databases.

Alternately, students could be required to complete an assignment in which they search for six periodical articles on a semester research topic by using at least three subject-specific databases. They will submit printouts of the database records with subject terms circled; printouts of each periodical's bibliographic record from the online catalog; a photocopy or printout of the first page of each article found; a list of citations to each article in proper format followed by an analysis of why that article is or is not relevant to their topic; and finally, a comparison of the scope and the types of citations found in each database.

DATABASE DESCRIPTION AND USABILITY

There is nothing like hands-on practice using a database to figure out how it works. Teaching others how to use a database is also a good way to enhance learning.

Goal: In exercise 39 students will gain an in-depth understanding of one indexing and abstracting database and a familiarity with several more. Students will learn the basic characteristics and features of many of the databases they will be using throughout their academic careers. The common characteristics of all databases will emerge, further empowering students to learn on their own in the future.

Description: For this project, students work in teams of three or four to investigate a particular subject-specific indexing and abstracting database assigned by the instructor. The students are guided by a worksheet that asks specific questions. They have a certain amount of time to discover the database, after which they are expected to teach the database to the entire class in a presentation of ten to fifteen minutes. Students are encouraged to use visual aids such as posters and handouts to enhance the quality of their presentation. Each group is graded on a number of criteria by the other members of the class and by the instructor. Criteria include the group's effectiveness in presenting the overall description and scope of the database; examples of basic searches and features; examples of advanced

searches and features; and proper determination of the audience for the database, that is, who would use it. Students' final grade on the project is a combination of the grades given by their peers and those given by the instructor.

Tips for conducting the exercise: Students should be given some time during one or more class meetings to work on this project. They will also need to get together outside of class to organize their presentation, come up with sample searches, design visual aids and handouts, and so forth—a fact that should be emphasized. This project is a fair amount of work, and the instructor's expectations should be made clear. Based on particular teaching situations, the amount of class time students can be given to discover their databases will vary, as will the time between starting the project and giving the class presentations. In terms of presentation, students sometimes enjoy having a role set for them in which to frame the presentation of the information. You can set up a scenario, for example, making each group a "sales team" from the database's parent company who are trying to sell a subscription to the database to the university. This gives them some incentive to make the presentation interesting and helps students who are shy about getting up in front of the class as themselves.

This exercise addresses ACRL Standard 2, Performance Indicator 1.

This chapter has provided an overview of the universe of information student researchers will encounter in periodical publications and of the tools researchers use to identify information relevant to their needs within this ever-expanding universe.

One aspect of this search for periodical information that was not emphasized was how to actually find the articles identified. Therefore, if possible, supplement the exercises presented in this chapter with a full discussion of how to physically locate the information identified, including using the library catalog to determine if the library (or other libraries in a consortium) owns the periodical and, if so, where it is shelved. Include alternatives for obtaining the article, such as interlibrary loan or visiting other local libraries.

Notes

1. John Feather and Paul Sturges, eds., *International Encyclopedia of Information and Library Science* (London: Routledge, 1997).

2. Carla J. List, *Information Research*, 2nd ed. (Dubuque, IA: Kendall/Hunt, 2002), 40.

Database Discovery Project

Groups of three to four students will be assigned a specific database. Your team will have [this class period] to discover the features of the database and learn how to use it. During our [next] class meeting [date], all teams will teach the rest of the class how to use their databases. Each team will produce an original fact sheet or user guide. Each team's "Database Discovery Project" presentation will be evaluated by the team's classmates as well as the instructor. Your final grade will be a combination of these grades.

Your presentation should take approximately ten to fifteen minutes. Every team member is required to actively participate in their group's presentation. If you want to do well on this project, be prepared to meet with your team outside of class to prepare your presentation and any visual aids or handouts that you will be using. The "Database Discovery Project" worksheet below will guide you in your discovery and help you structure your presentation.

A successful presentation will

- include information on the database's content, design, time period covered, audience, search capabilities (basic and advanced), and retrieval options

- include demonstrations and discussion of each item listed above and completely address the questions in parts 1 and 2 of the "Database Discovery Project" worksheet below

- be flexible—you should be able to explain any unexpected search results or problems that might crop up during your presentation and to recover from them if they occur

- include attractive and informative visual aids and handouts

Suggestion: Find the Help or About or news screens for the database. This is where you can find many of the answers to the following questions.

Part 1: Database Description

What is the name of your database?

What organization is responsible for providing access to the database? (This is often called the "database vendor.")

What is the name of the software created by this vendor for searching the database? (This is like a brand name for the screen interface.)

What organization is responsible for creating the database? Is this the same or different from the database vendor?

Hint: Often a database will be created by a professional association. For example, the American Economic Association creates the database EconLit. EconLit is then offered to subscribers through different vendors, each with its own interface. So a library can subscribe to EconLit through the organization OCLC, which calls its search interface FirstSearch. Or it is possible to subscribe to EconLit through the company Cambridge Scientific Abstracts. This organization calls its search interface CSA Internet Database Service. Yet another vendor that carries EconLit is EBSCO Information Services, through its software named EBSCOhost.

Find an overview or explanation of the database. Tell us what the database is all about.

What subject areas or disciplines does the database cover?

Who do you think would be the most likely users of this database? Think of as many different groups as you can and list them in order of most likely to use. Explain your answer.

Try to find out how big the database is. How many entries, or records, does the database contain? What does this mean?

(cont.)

What types of materials are included as sources in the database? (Books, book chapters, journal articles, magazine articles, newspaper articles, conference proceedings, patents, websites, government publications, and so on.)

How many different sources does the database index? Give an example of two or three titles.

What time period or years does the database cover? What does this mean?

Are the sources indexed in the database all English-language sources? If not, what other languages are included?

Does the database provide the full text or content of the articles it indexes? If so, does it provide the full text for all articles indexed?

If the database does not provide full text, then what does it give you? Explain and describe.

How often is the database updated (that is, how often are new records added)?

Part 2: Database Usability

Find the database's Help or User Guide screens. How do they work? What do they include? Is the help easy or difficult to understand? Do you think it is helpful? What is most helpful in the Help section?

Does the database use a "controlled vocabulary?" (If you aren't sure what this is, take a look at your class notes or the glossary in the back of your textbook.) Is there a Subject Thesaurus or a Subject Terms list? Find out and be able to explain what it is and demonstrate how to use it. How easy is it to use?

How does one search this database?

Is it user-friendly or difficult to figure out?

By what access points does the database allow you to search?

Be able to demonstrate and describe several methods for searching the database.

Does the database offer advanced search mechanisms? Be able to demonstrate and describe any.

What fields are included in the full record for an item? Show us a record and identify the fields.

Does the database offer Boolean searching? Be able to demonstrate how to set up a Boolean search.

Explain all of the different ways that information from the database can be retrieved (for example, by marking records, reformatting records, printing records, e-mailing records, and saving records).

In preparation for your presentation, be sure to take clear and comprehensive notes while you are in database-discovery mode. For example, write down the path to any Help screens you might want to show the class. Note any searches you did that would be especially useful in demonstrating the database's features.

Chapter Eight

The Web and Scholarly Research

Although many of today's students spend a great deal of time surfing the Web and consider themselves savvy web searchers, others have had very little experience with it. Not surprisingly, differences in students' levels of experience often fall along the lines of economic background, race, and age. For this reason, when teaching the Web as a research tool, it is important to start with the basics. What exactly is the Internet? What is the history of the Internet? Who can put information up on the Web, and how? And what is the World Wide Web specifically, in comparison to the Internet as a whole? Just a brief outline of the technology of the Internet in the simplest terms will benefit all students, not only those who are inexperienced.

In the context of information literacy, it is of great importance to go into some detail about where the information on the Web comes from. Who creates it? What kind of organizations and individuals publish information to the World Wide Web? Who is their intended audience? What is their purpose? How is their purpose likely to affect the information they provide?

Just as students learned to differentiate between general, trade, and scholarly periodicals, they should understand the difference between the types and orientation of information found on the sites of government agencies (.gov) such as the Census Bureau or the Bureau of Justice Statistics; educational institutions (.edu) such as universities and some research institutions and museums such as the Smithsonian Institute; organizations or associations (.org), including issue-based organizations like the American Civil Liberties Union or the NAACP; and industry and professional associations like the Toy Industry Association or the American Medical Association. In addition, there is what is now the largest category of websites, commercial sites (.com) that exist to advertise or sell a product or service.

Many students use websites as information sources for high school and college assignments. In fact, search engines such as Google are often the first place they turn when faced with a research project. They often seem unaware of the rich variety and depth of information resources available through their school, college or university, and public libraries that are simply unavailable on the Web. Librarians hear directly from teachers and professors who are unhappy with the quality of information students are using, or they hear through the students that their instructors have arbitrarily ruled that they are "not allowed to use any information from the Internet."

This again stresses the importance, emphasized throughout these chapters, that students must learn to critically evaluate the quality of the information they find so that they can make intelligent decisions about whether or not it is appropriate for academic use. Nowhere is this more true than for information they find on the Web.

SEARCHING THE WORLD WIDE WEB

After a general introduction to the Internet, students should learn about searching the Web in some depth, just as they learned what goes on "behind the screen" of indexing and abstracting databases in chapter 7. Most students know how to go to Yahoo!, Google, Ask.com, or any number of sites for searching the Internet and type in a few words related to what they want to find. They need to learn that each of these Internet search tools has its own strengths and weaknesses, methods of indexing, and advanced search capabilities.

Students should learn some of the specifics of these sites for searching the Web. For example, web directories are organized by people who select the sites to be included, and web search engines are compiled by computer programs known as "spiders" or "crawlers" that crawl through the Web, indexing sites according to preprogrammed algorithms. Some search engines index the words in the title of the web page only, while some index the title and the lead paragraphs, and others the entire page. The databases of different search engines are refreshed periodically, and the frequency that they are refreshed will affect search results. The relative size of the major search engines and directories varies widely. Search engines rank web pages based on different criteria. An excellent source of this kind of information for instructors and students is the website Search Engine Watch.[1]

Web directories and search engines, like library databases, have Help screens that will explain how to search most effectively. These screens will outline the search syntax of the site and any advanced search features. For example, is Boolean searching supported? How do you search for a phrase? Does the search engine assume that there is an *and* between your search terms? Will the search *Italian recipes* find information on the concept "Italian recipes," or will it find pages with either word anywhere in the page? Does it matter if you type *Italian* or *italian*? Can you limit your search, for example, to have the search engine only show results from the .gov domain?

Specialty search engines are available, for example, those designed to find results in a particular subject area, such as law or health, and multimedia search engines that allow one to search only for sound, image, or video files. There are also search engines called "metacrawlers," which allow a search to be sent to several search engines at once, with the results appearing on one page.

These are but some of the many factors that will affect the outcome of students' web searches. Searchers' understanding of how to structure a search according to the characteristics of the particular search tool will allow them more control over the search and will produce better results.

THE LIBRARY DATABASE VERSUS THE WEB

Many students have no idea of the amounts and types of information they miss when they use only the Web for research. Although libraries offer carefully chosen collections of high-quality information—often available via the Internet—students do not understand that often this information is proprietary and not freely available. Students need to learn the differences in the quality of what is freely available on the Web and what is provided by subscription for academic purposes with restricted access. They need to understand the appropriate uses and caveats for each source of information.

Goal: In exercise 40 students will experience the differences between information found in periodical articles accessed through the library's general indexing and abstracting database, and the information found through searching the Web using a directory or search engine. The instructor can take this opportunity to prove to students that in most cases, a library database will yield more information-rich results with less time and effort than conducting the same search on the Web. A second goal is to familiarize students with web search tools.

Description: Students work in teams of two or three people. Each team receives an index card containing a specific topic and related questions. Two teams in the room receive the same topic. Students follow the worksheet below to search for the answer to their questions, using the library's general periodicals database, a web directory, and a search engine. Then, of the sources they find, each team will identify the one that they believe best answers their questions while also being the most reputable source, and they will decide whether they would use that source for a college-level research assignment. Each team will share their source with the rest of the class, which will decide which of the sources found by each team on the same topic is better and why.

Tips for conducting the exercise: Select topics for which it will be relatively easy to find information in both a general periodicals database and on the Web. Picking topics that might be more likely to have "far-out" information on the Web, such as "extraterrestrials," can highlight the difference between information found in a library periodical database and on the Internet. Here are some examples of topics that have been used for this exercise:

Drug testing in the workplace (How common is it? Are there any problems with this practice?)

Breast cancer (What are the available treatments? Are there any new treatments on the horizon? If so, which are most promising?)

Extraterrestrials (How likely is it that intelligent life exists somewhere in the universe besides the planet Earth? What do scientists think about this issue?)

This exercise addresses ACRL Standard 1, Performance Indicators 1, 2, and 4; Standard 2, Performance Indicators 2 and 3; Standard 3, Performance Indicators 2, 4, and 6; and Standard 5, Performance Indicator 1.

STRATEGIES FOR SEARCHING THE INTERNET

In preparation for the next exercise in this chapter, and as a logical follow-up to the randomness of the search results students may have encountered in the last exercise, it is a good idea to present students with a set of general strategies that will help them find information on the Web.

Who Would Know?

Before beginning a search, researchers should consider where the information they are looking for would most likely be found. Who would be an authoritative source on the topic? For example, if the researchers want to know the weather in Chicago, they could go to Yahoo! and search for "weather and Chicago," but they might have to wade through a large number of irrelevant and unhelpful results. On the other hand, if the researchers directly consulted the Weather Channel site, at http://weather.com, it would take only seconds to find out the weather for the Windy City. Likewise, if students wanted to know how many murders were committed in the United States last year, they could enter "murders and United States and [year]" into Alta Vista and face a long list of results. Or the researchers could first ask a librarian or think about who collects crime statistics nationwide. Searching Alta Vista for the "Bureau of Justice Statistics" will quickly lead to that site, which has the desired information.

USE SEARCHING SKILLS

Earlier chapters presented exercises for teaching students how to break down a research question into key concepts, come up with a list of possible synonyms for each potential search term, and then formulate a search statement that would be understood by library indexing and abstracting databases. Students should be reminded of these skills they have already acquired and be informed that such skills can also be applied to searching the Internet.

Know Your Web Search Tool

For the best search results, students should know the basic characteristics of their web search tool and how to most effectively enter their search, given the requirements of that site.

Remember What Is Not Available on the Internet

The Internet contains a wealth of information, some of it high quality from reputable sources and some of it low quality from questionable sources. However, we owe it to students to make them truly understand that there is a great deal of information that they will not find online. In fact, a recent *New York Times* article noted that a Google search, despite being able to "see" a trillion websites with unique URLs, was only scratching the surface of the information that actually exists on the Web.[2] Furthermore, much has been written about the "Invisible Web," or "Deep Web," which

Should I Use a Library Database, or Should I Just Search the Web?

For this exercise, you will work in teams of two or three. Each team will receive an index card containing a specific topic and related questions. One other team in the classroom will receive the same topic as your team. You will be competing with them to see which of you can find the highest quality, most reliable sources that answer or address your questions.

Look up your topic in the web search tool or library database indicated below and describe the results of your searches as prompted. As you note how each search tool or database responds to your query, don't forget to actually find the answer to your question, noting sources (either articles or websites) that have the information you need. When you are finished, you will select one source from those you found that best answers your question and appears to be a high-quality, reputable source.

Be prepared to share your favorite source and how you found it with the class. Would you use this source for a college-level research assignment?

WEB SEARCH TOOL OR REFERENCE DATABASE	HOW DID YOU ENTER YOUR SEARCH? (Be exact.)	NUMBER OF HITS	HOW ARE YOUR RESULTS ORGANIZED? (e.g., chronologically, by relevance, etc.)	WHAT TYPES OF MATERIALS DID YOU FIND? (e.g., web pages, periodical articles, studies; from which domain type; etc.)
Google (www.google.com)				
Bing (www.bing.com)				
[Library's general periodical database]				

The Best Sources Found

URL (Web Address) OR PATH (You may wish to bookmark the sites and articles you find, because you will need to get back to your favorites to show the class.)	DESCRIPTION OF INFORMATION FOUND AND WHO WROTE IT

contains information that cannot be indexed by search engines because it is hidden within databases.

Search tools such as library indexing and abstracting services are not available on the Web to just anyone; institutions or individuals must subscribe to them to gain access. In general, students should be aware that any proprietary or copyrighted information is not generally available online for free, at least not legally. A good rule of thumb is that if an information resource costs money in print format, it probably costs money on the Web too, if it is also available there.

SEARCHING SAVVY ON THE INTERNET

Contributed by Amanda K. Izenstark

The Web offers tremendous opportunities for discovery, but when it comes to Internet searching, few users go beyond the basic search screens. As a foundation, students should know about an array of search tools and understand the specific features that will help them effectively target searches.

Other tools can help students become savvy information consumers, but only if they know how to find them and harness their information. Knowing how to find relevant blogs and harvest pertinent postings is one step in this process.

So Many Search Engines

Google is currently the most popular search engine, but it hasn't always been (AltaVista and AllTheWeb once also roamed the Net). Competitors continue to emerge from the ether to offer alternatives for searching the general Web. Other tools may have subject strengths that users never discover. Knowing more than just one tool can help users develop more sophisticated search strategies and have a clearer understanding of why they receive the results they do.

Goal: In exercise 41 students will explore the basic and advanced features of an assigned search engine. This exercise will introduce students to tools that have other features and perhaps a different scope from the tools they currently use.

Description: Small groups of students will explore an assigned search engine's basic search, advanced search, and other features. Students will present their search tools and findings to the class and compare their findings to the results and functionality of their usual search tools. Sharing results will provide the opportunity for students to learn about tools other than the one investigated for this exercise.

Tips for conducting the exercise: Before the session, explain and demonstrate some of the advanced features of the search engine(s) students are most likely to be familiar with already. Then, locate alternate search engines freely available on the open Web, and select one site for every two students. Students will need computers with Internet access. Some examples as of this writing include Bing (www.bing.com), Clusty

(www.clusty.com), Blinkx (www.blinkx.com), and Scirus (www.scirus.com).

This exercise addresses ACRL Standard 2, Performance Indicators 3, 4, and 5.

Blogs, RSS Feeds, and Feed Readers

Weblogs (aka blogs) became popular at the end of the 1990s, and they remain a subset of the Web where

---

Exercise 41

Search Engine Extravaganza

For this exercise, you will work in teams of two. Answer the questions below, and be prepared to share your results with the class. If you are not sure of a topic to use as a sample search, any of your research topics will make for excellent sample searches.

1. What is the name and URL of your search engine?
2. Where can you get help? (Is it easy to find, and is it really helpful?)
3. How does the basic search work? (Does it use Boolean? Natural language? Something else?) Please give us an example.
4. Is there an advanced search? How does it work? What are some of its features? Please have an example that makes good use of some of the advanced features! (Make sure the advanced search is searching the same content the basic search searches!)
5. What kind of results did you get? (Web pages, PDF files, news groups, images, or something else?)
6. Can you tell why your results show up in the order that they do—is it date, relevance, or something else?
7. Do your results change if you change the order of your search terms?
8. Does this tool perform a general web search, or is it more specialized?
9. Are there any unique or special features that make this search engine better than others? When might you want to use this tool over the most popular search engine(s)?

much topical discussion takes place. Blogs are informal means of discussing new developments in a field from many different perspectives.

Feed readers can help students turn their information seeking into information harvesting. Feed readers allow users to create a customizable and centralized list of links that automatically aggregate news or blog posts as they occur. In addition, when RSS feeds are provided by database publishers, the feeds can be used to display new articles on a topic.

Some feed readers are web based (optimal for those who use more than one computer on a regular basis), while others work as browser plug-ins or separate programs. Most modern browsers (Firefox, Internet Explorer, Safari, etc.) include some minimal feed-reading capabilities, but for more functionality, other tools are recommended. As of this writing, Google Reader and NetVibes are popular web-based readers, and Sage is a popular Firefox plug-in. Depending on a class's comfort with technology, students can be given a list of readers to explore and evaluate in relation to their information needs, or one reader could be recommended for the whole class.

Keeping Up: Blogging

Students in advanced classes can use blogs written by journalists, researchers, and/or practitioners to follow new developments in their fields. Incorporating this activity may aid job seekers who might be required to show their knowledge of the field in upcoming interviews or at job fairs.

Goal: In exercise 42, students will locate blogs on their topics or in their current or anticipated fields and, with the addition of the optional question, locate RSS feeds that they can include in a feed reader. This exercise will introduce students to additional web tools they can use to locate and harvest information.

Description: For this exercise, have students use the blog search tool(s) of their choice to look for blogs related to their research topics, majors, or careers.

Tips for conducting the exercise: In advance, describe blogs and briefly demonstrate how to search for blogs. If incorporating feed readers into the exercise, also demonstrate how to determine whether a site offers an RSS feed. It also may be helpful to provide a list of blog search tools to students before they start the exercise. Some examples as of this writing include Google Blog Search (http://blogsearch.google.com), Technorati (http://technorati.com), and Ask.com Blogsearch (http://blogsearch.ask.com). A general Internet search for "blog search" will produce other options as well.

This exercise addresses ACRL Standard 2, Performance Indicators 1, 2, 3, and 5, and Standard 3, Performance Indicator 2.

Exercise 42

Finding and Following Blogs on a Topic

You have just started an internship at the company of your dreams, and one of your tasks is to monitor information newly published on the Internet about the field you're working in and share that information with your supervisor. Doing this will not only help you fulfill the requirements of your position but will also keep you abreast of developing trends as you start your job hunt.

First, select a blog search tool to use. Look at and use the features and functionality of the tool to help you perform a targeted search. Can you limit your search by domain, for example? Does the search tool offer an "alert" or "update" option that saves your search and notifies you of new posts on your topic?

Next, search for blogs that relate to your topic, major, or career. Investigate the topics of each blog, and locate the author's (or authors') credentials if possible.

Narrow down your search to your top three blogs. What criteria have you used to evaluate the blogs you selected? What features led these to become your top three? Summarize your search strategies and findings, and be prepared to share them with the class.

Optional additional question: Do the blogs you've selected offer RSS feeds?

Using a feed reader can help the twenty-first-century researcher stay up-to-date on a topic with little effort.

Keeping Up: Feed Readers

Many publications have an online presence that includes regularly updated columns. Locating these resources and showing students how to import the pages' RSS feeds into a feed reader will help those who want to know the latest news without having to remember to check a site regularly.

Goal: In exercise 43, students will investigate web-based and downloadable feed readers and select a tool that meets their information needs. They will then add feeds from the blogs they found in exercise 42 to their feed readers.

Description: For this exercise, students will need to know how to identify RSS feeds on blogs and in databases.

Tips for conducting the exercise: It may be helpful to provide students with a list of feed readers to investigate in advance, including web-based, browser-based, and downloadable feed readers for current operating systems. This assignment may require that students have their own computers available, as they may need to install client software. If this is not possible, limit the list to web-based feed readers and adapt the exercise as necessary.

This exercise addresses ACRL Standard 2, Performance Indicator 5.

Exercise 43

Following Blogs Using Feed Readers

Feed readers can help you manage the flow of information on your topic and keep you updated on new developments with minimal effort on your part. For this exercise, examine at least two feed readers for eventual continued use in the future.

Topics to consider when evaluating a feed reader:

1. Do you always use the same computer, or do you use multiple computers?

2. Do you want or need to make "folders" or use "labels" to manage your incoming information? Does the feed reader offer this function?

3. Can you save postings for reading at a later time?

4. Can you e-mail posts to other people?

5. How easy is the feed reader to use overall?

Which feed readers did you evaluate?

Which functions are most important to you?

Be prepared to share your findings—and your opinions regarding your preferred feed reader—with the class.

INFORMATION ON THE WEB

There is no place where evaluation is more relevant than in examining information found on the Web. This is because anyone can create a website. Most web pages do not undergo any sort of editorial review process, as do books and periodical articles. Therefore, critical-thinking skills and an active, questioning mind are needed to evaluate any information found on the Internet.

Criteria for Evaluating Web Information

Purpose of the site and intended audience

- Are the goals of the author stated? Is there a statement of scope, target audience, or purpose?
- Who is the site designed for? What audience is the site's author trying to reach?
- Is the site scholarly or popular?
- Does the site contain advertising? What might this tell you?
- What is the overall purpose of the site? To inform? Persuade or advocate? Entertain? Sell a product?

Authority and credibility of author

- Can the author of the site be identified? Is it clear who has ultimate responsibility for the content of the material, whether it be an individual or an organization?
- Is contact information given so that you can get in touch with the author or organization for clarification or more information?
- What are the author's qualifications? Does he or she list his or her occupation, years of experience, position, or education?
- Do you think the author has expertise on the subject?
- What is the author's institutional affiliation, if any? Is the author affiliated with an educational institution? A nonprofit organization? A company?
- What is the domain of the site (.edu, .gov, .org, .com)? Is it an academic, governmental, organizational, commercial, or personal site? From what country does it originate?
- Is this site connected to an organization of any sort? If so, what is the mission of this organization?

Accuracy and reliability of the information on the site

- Does the site appear to be well researched?
- Are there references to sources of information supporting any statements made or viewpoints held?
- Is statistical information labeled clearly and easy to read?
- Are the sources for any factual or statistical information documented so that they can be verified in another source?
- What method of data collection or research was used by the author (if applicable)?
- Does the site include grammatical, spelling, or typographical errors?
- How does the site compare to print information resources available on this topic?
- If links to other sites are listed, are they quality sites?

Currency and timeliness of the information on the site

- When was this information published? Does the page list the date it was created?
- Does the page indicate when it was last updated?
- Are there any "dead" links—that is, links to other sites that no longer work?

Objectivity or bias of the site

- Are the goals of the author clearly stated? Is there a statement of scope, target audience, or purpose?
- Does the site present many opinions on the topic or only one?
- Can you tell if the site contains mostly opinions or facts?
- Can you identify any bias in the information and opinions provided?

- Is the site sponsored by a company or organization?
- Does the site reflect the agenda of a political, religious, or social group or institution?
- If there is advertising on the site, is it clearly differentiated from the informational content?

Structure and navigation of the site

- Is the organization of the site easy to understand? Is it clear and logical?
- Is it easy to navigate between different parts of the site?
- Is there a link to return to the first page of the site, the home page?
- Does the site offer a table of contents or a site index?
- Does the site offer a search box?
- Do graphics on the site add to or detract from the site itself?

Conclusion

- Is this site a reliable, well-documented source of information from a reputable author or organization?
- Would this be a good source of information for a research paper?

INFORMATION ON THE WEB—EVALUATION AND COMPARISON

Information on the Web is not always written by an expert. Sometimes information on the Web is not entirely accurate. Even worse, sometimes the information on the Web is not even true! A wise web user will always question the source and quality of information found on the open Web.

Goal: In exercise 44 students will also be made aware that there is some very highly questionable information on the Internet that often masquerades as legitimate. They will learn to identify quality information and spot the differences between "good" and "bad" information.

Description: The instructor selects pairs of websites related to the same topic. One site is legitimate: it is a reputable site that could be used as a quality source

for a research project. The other site is of questionable quality. Students are divided into teams of two for this exercise. Each team gets one website, so that two teams are working on the same topic. One team has the reputable site and another has the site of questionable quality. Students spend twenty or thirty minutes evaluating their sites, using the "Criteria for Evaluating Web Information" above. Then each team shows its site to the rest of the class and explains its evaluation of the site, pointing to evidence on the site that supports the team's view.

Tips for conducting the exercise: Topics and sites that have been used for this exercise follow.

Martin Luther King Jr.

Martin Luther King Jr.: A Historical Examination, at www.martin lutherking.org

The Martin Luther King Jr. Papers Project, at http://mlk-kpp01 .stanford.edu

UFOs

CAUS: Citizens Against UFO Secrecy, at www.v-j-enterprises .com/caus.html

SETI Institute, at www.seti-inst.edu

Greenhouse Effect

CO_2 and Climate Resource Center, at www.greeningearthsociety.org

---

Exercise 44

Evaluation of Information on the Web

For this exercise, you will work in teams of two. Each team will receive an index card with the address of a website on it. You will have approximately twenty to thirty minutes to complete this exercise.

Go to the website and explore it thoroughly; then evaluate the site using the "Criteria for Evaluating Web Information" discussed earlier. On a piece of paper, note the title and URL of your site and summarize your conclusions about the site's quality, noting specific evidence that supports your evaluation. Please be prepared to share your site and your evaluation of it with the class.

EPA Global Warming Site, at http://yosemite.epa.gov/oar/globalwarming.nsf/content/index.html

Many sites created by librarians have lists of websites that are very good for this type of assignment.[3]

This exercise addresses ACRL Standard 1, Performance Indicators 1, 2, and 4; Standard 2, Performance Indicator 2; Standard 3, Performance Indicators 2, 4, 5, and 6; and Standard 5, Performance Indicator 1.

EVERYTHING IS ON THE WEB?

A huge amount of information is simply not available via the Internet, for free or for a fee. For example, "Only about 8 percent of all journals are on the Web, and an even smaller fraction of books."[4] This is especially the case with older information. Some of the classics of world literature have been made available on scholarly websites such as Project Gutenberg,[5] but those are but a tiny fraction of the written works of humankind, most of which sit in obscurity on the shelves of libraries and rare-book rooms worldwide. In addition, the explosion of electronic information over the past few decades means that there are electronic archives, research datasets, and personal and organizational records "out there" that may never be preserved, not to mention made public.

The significance of all of this to researchers is that although the Internet can be an excellent place to conduct research, relying on it exclusively will mean missing a great deal of valuable information.

Here is another way of approaching web evaluation that allows the students to identify the most important criteria for evaluating websites for themselves.

Goal: In exercise 45 students will investigate assigned websites in order to develop their own set of evaluation criteria for quality or "worthy" websites.

Description:

Step 1: The instructor may introduce the session by sharing a story of a recent experience in web searching—perhaps a young neighbor of middle-school age has asked for guidance in finding websites for a school project or an elderly relative wants to search for websites about a medical ailment.

Step 2: Tell the class that you would like their help in developing a set of criteria for evaluating quality or "worthy" websites that you can pass along to other stu-

dents, and especially to your neighbor and the elderly relative.

Step 3: Pairs, or small groups of students, receive an index card with one website address written on it that they need to review. There are a total of four tasks to accomplish and a suggested length of time for doing each task (adjust time as needed).

Step 4: As students begin step 3, begin a short discussion of what they hope to find in a website that they trust—for the middle-school student or the elderly relative—or for their own school projects and papers. Ask them to consider what they think a website needs to do to prove its worth.

Step 5: At the end of their investigations, the groups report to the class by showing their website (either at their computer work station or by using a classroom computer broadcast system) and sharing a brief description of the site. While the students report on their work, ask for a volunteer to record the various criteria announced from each group.

Step 6: The class reviews the list together and formalizes the most important criteria to develop a class list of web-evaluation criteria.

Step 7: Compare the class list with web-evaluation sites that you are familiar with, such as Susan E. Beck's The Good, the Bad, and the Ugly site, at http://lib.nmsu.edu/instruction/evalcrit.html.

We've included two lists of websites to use for this exercise:

List A equals fun, strange, or bizarre sites. Some of these will be obviously "wrong" to students, but it enables them to clarify what is "right" or what needs to be in a website that they would trust for good information.

List A

www.medical-library.net
http://home.inreach.com/kumbach/velcro.html
www.ladiesagainstfeminism.com
www.breatharian.com
www.dhmo.org
http://zapatopi.net/treeoctopus/
http://people.csail.mit.edu/rahimi/helmet/
www.martinlutherking.org
www.ihr.org
www.shorty.com/bonsaikitten/
www.thedogisland.com/index.html

List B offers pairs of consumer-health sites that you may use as comparison examples. These examples are

Website Worthiness

Task 1 (five minutes)
Take notes on your investigation of the website. Describe the website content in terms of who, what, where, why, and when.

Task 2 (ten minutes)
Investigate the website. What's "right" or "wrong" with the website? Look for clues by critically examining the who, what, where, why, and when information that is provided by the site. Use the format below to make notes on all that you find.

ELEMENT	"RIGHT STUFF"	"WRONG STUFF"
Who		
What		
Where		
Why		
When		
Other?		

Task 3 (ten minutes)

Consider what you found in terms of "right stuff" and "wrong stuff."

Develop a list of at least *five* evaluative criteria that you feel are necessary to judge a website's validity, worthiness, and credibility—so that you will always get the "right stuff."

List them in the chart below.

Next to each criterion that you list, describe what type of information you want to find from any website that will help you to determine if the website meets or does not meet the stated criteria.

EVALUATION CRITERIA	INFORMATION THAT WILL INFORM THE CRITERIA

Task 4 (five minutes)
Would you recommend this website? Be prepared to share with the class a description of this website, what is "right" and "wrong" with it, and the evaluation criteria that you have selected.

useful for students who have some experience in critical evaluation of information. We've used these successfully in a semester-long credit course after students have explored evaluation of encyclopedias, books, and articles.

List B

www.medical-library.net	*http://medlineplus.gov*
www.amfoundation.org	*http://nccam.nih.gov*
www.apjohncancerinstitute.org	*www.mdanderson.org*
www.braintumortreatment.org	*www.abta.org*
http://arthritiscure.org	*www.arthritis.org*

Tips for conducting the exercise: As the students work, the instructor should circulate among the groups. If you observe a group that is struggling with a task, make statements or ask a few questions that encourage critical thinking (e.g., describe what you see; give an example of what you are describing; give an example found in the website that supports what the assignment is asking you to do; what is it that looks "good" or "wrong"?).

This exercise addresses ACRL Standard 3, Performance Indicators 2, 4, and 5, and Standard 4, Performance Indicators 1, 2, and 3.

Notes

1. Search Engine Watch, Jupitermedia Corporation, 1996–2002, www.searchenginewatch.com.

2. Alex Wright, "Exploring a 'Deep Web' That Google Can't Grasp," *New York Times* 22 (February 2009), www.nytimes.com/2009/02/23/technology/internet/23search.html?_r=1&th&emc=th.

3. Librarians have created several sites offering links to websites of questionable quality for the purpose of instructing students about the pitfalls of web research. These sites include The Good, the Bad and the Ugly; or, Why It's a Good Idea to Evaluate Web Sources, by Susan E. Beck, http://lib.nmsu.edu/instruction/evalcrit.html.

4. Mark Y. Herring, "Ten Reasons Why the Internet Is No Substitute for a Library," *American Libraries* 32, no. 4 (April 2001): 76–78.

5. Project Gutenberg Official Home Site, Project Gutenberg and PROMO.NET, 1971–2002, http://gutenberg.net.

Chapter Nine

Other Tools for Research

When students receive a research assignment, they tend to use resources they already know: reference books, journal articles, and websites. They are frequently familiar with some or all of these sources and know that there is someone in the library who can help them locate and use other sources of information of the same kind.

EXPERTS AND ORGANIZATIONS

What does not come to mind so easily are human sources of information. There is a wealth of human knowledge and expertise on every college campus, in organizations throughout the world, and in local communities. For almost any topic imaginable, there exists a professional, trade, or special-interest organization.

An example of a professional organization is the American Medical Association (AMA), whose members are doctors. The AMA provides professional information and networking opportunities to its members, educates the public and policy makers about health issues, and advocates for the interests of the medical community.

An example of a trade organization is the National Restaurant Association. This group is made up of individual restaurant owners and restaurant chains. Their goal is to represent, educate, and promote the restaurant industry and to advocate for governmental policies favorable to the industry.

An example of a special-interest organization is the Surfrider Foundation, which is a nonprofit organization dedicated to protecting our oceans, waves, and beaches. Other examples of special-interest organizations are the National Organization for Women, the NAACP, the American Civil Libraries Union, and Greenpeace.

IDENTIFICATION OF EXPERTS AND ORGANIZATIONS

How do students identify an appropriate expert or association? One method of identifying experts is to use a reference directory such as the *Encyclopedia of*

Associations. This encyclopedia is indexed by the title and keyword for each organization. Entries show contact information and the scope of the organizations' activities. It is helpful to note that not all associations make information freely available to the public. Many limit information to members only.

Goal: In exercise 46 students will learn to identify experts and organizations that can provide information about a specific topic.

Description: For this exercise, have students use a directory of associations in print format or online. Students will identify individuals and organizations appropriate to their Paper Trail Project topic (see exercise 50) or to the instructor's assigned topic. The exercise may simply familiarize students with this type of directory or may instruct students to contact their chosen organizations and ask for information to be sent to them.

Tips for conducting the exercise: We have used the *Encyclopedia of Associations* and its online counterpart, *Associations Unlimited.* Any similar directory will work.

This exercise addresses ACRL Standard 2, Performance Indicators 1, 2, and 3.

Statistics

Another type of information that can be useful in research is statistics. Statistics are facts and data. Statistics is also the science that deals with collection, classification, analysis, and interpretation of facts or data. Our world is filled with statistics. Every individual in the United States is counted in the census, has a Social Security number, lives in a ZIP code area, has an account of one sort or another, goes to school, has a flu shot, registers a car, or becomes a statistic in some other way. The U.S. government is the largest compiler of statistical information in the world. Many other groups and individuals collect statistics as well.

Types of Statistics

Descriptive statistics use numbers to summarize the information collected concerning a particular situation. For example, a random sample of students was taken at a university campus in Providence, Rhode Island. Of those questioned, 15 percent used Five Star notebooks for their course note taking. This descriptive statistic is a kind of shorthand for what actually happened. One hundred and forty students at the university campus in Providence, Rhode Island, were

asked what kind of notebook they used for note taking. Twenty-one of those students used Five Star notebooks. Doing the math required to change these numbers into a percentage resulted in the descriptive statistic above.

Statistical inference is the use of numbers to make generalizations or predictions about what a large group of people will do based on what a smaller group of people did. For example, using the raw data above (of 140 Rhode Island students, 21 use Five Star notebooks; thus, 15 percent use Five Star notebooks), statistical inference might claim that on the basis of the information collected, 15 percent of all university students in New England's capital cities use Five Star notebooks.

This statistic implies that students in New England's capital cities use Five Star notebooks, even though students in only one New England capital city were ques-

Exercise 46

Finding Experts and Organizations

For this assignment you may use either the print copy of the *Encyclopedia of Associations* or the web version, which can be found on the Library Web Resources list under the title *Associations Unlimited.*

Look through the listings and select three experts or organizations most closely related to your topic. Report the information in the format requested below, giving specific information for each expert or organization.

Name of Expert or Organization: _____

Contact Information: _____

Web Address: _____

Description of What the Expert or Organization Does (scope): _____

Now go to the website for each expert or association. Is there any relevant information there? Print it out and attach it to this worksheet or describe it on the back of this page.

Contact one expert or organization, using phone, mail, e-mail, or fax, and ask them to send you information on your topic. Or create a list of short questions you'd like your expert or association to address. Attach the contact information and the list of questions (if relevant) to the response you receive.

tioned. Statistical inference might use the Providence statistic to infer something about a larger population. Claims made through statistical inference must be examined very carefully for accuracy and probability. There may be forces at work in Providence causing university students there to buy Five Star notebooks that do not extend to all New England cities. To infer that what happens in Providence happens elsewhere in New England may be inaccurate or even incorrect. The sample size for the study of notebook use was fairly small—only 140 students were questioned. It might be that those students all live in the vicinity of the same mall that carries Five Star notebooks. Or perhaps the students surveyed were all contacted at the same time of day. Those students taking day classes might have different options for purchasing Five Star notebooks than those who attend classes at night. A survey of a larger number of people over a longer period of time might give very different results, which would then change what could be inferred from the statistic collected.

Where Do Statistics Come From?

The U.S. government is the largest collector and compiler of statistics in the world. Government agencies collect their own statistics. For example, the Census Bureau, the Bureau of Economic Analysis, the Bureau of Labor Statistics, the National Center for Education Statistics, the Bureau of Justice Statistics, the National Center for Health Statistics, and the Bureau of Transportation Statistics are all government agencies specializing in the collection of statistics.

In the international community, there are intergovernmental organizations that collect data as well. For example, the United Nations, the World Bank/International Monetary Fund, and the Organization for Economic Cooperation and Development (OECD) are all intergovernmental agencies cooperating to collect data on a global scale.

Professional, trade, and special-interest organizations also collect statistics. The American Library Association, the American Medical Association, the American Marketing Association, the American Bar Association, the Beer Institute, Amnesty International, Greenpeace, and the Toy Industry Association all are organizations that collect statistics.

There are also agencies, researchers, and individuals that collect statistics for various purposes. These groups or individuals tend to focus on specific topics, such as attitudes of high school students toward drug use, whether the death penalty should be abolished, how popular the president of the United States is, or what the most-watched shows on television are. Much research and data collection are done at universities or research institutes or by opinion research firms. Results are reported in scholarly publications like journals and, in some cases, in the public media.

Strategies for Finding Statistical Information

When looking for statistical information, it is important to look for some key facts. The first question to ask is, Who would collect this information? For example, if we were looking for statistics on how many people were put to death in the United States last year under the death penalty laws, it would be necessary to consider what organization or department of the government might gather and publish that statistic. The death penalty is administered at the state level, so it might be possible to check every state, but perhaps there is one place where the information is compiled. The federal government is likely to collect and compile the statistics from the states concerning the number of people put to death under the death penalty laws. What part of the federal government might do this? The department in charge of law enforcement might be a good place to start, so the Department of Justice is the logical place. This department has a Bureau of Justice Statistics. Although an individual may not know of the existence of this bureau, by following a logical thought process and looking for the existence of such a department or division, it should not be too difficult to find the name of an appropriate agency. Many U.S. government agencies and departments have websites, and they are all listed in various government manuals.

Another possibility for finding this statistic would be to identify an organization either in support of or in opposition to the death penalty. These organizations would be sure to have the statistic, although it might be important to watch for possible manipulation in how they report or use that statistic. In fact, it might be a good idea to get the same statistic from more than one source to ensure the reliability of the number. Organizations in favor of or against a certain cause are likely to be listed in the *Encyclopedia of Associations*.

Finally, it might be possible to find up-to-date statistics in a newspaper or magazine article about the death penalty. Newspaper indexes are available in most libraries in paper, microform, or online formats.

USING STATISTICAL SOURCES

Obtaining statistical information can be a useful part of the research process. However, like other types of information, statistical information must be evaluated. Students should become familiar with various reliable sources of statistics and learn to think about who might collect the statistics they may need.

Goal: Exercise 47 will familiarize students with sources of statistical information.

Description: In this exercise students will use selected sources of statistical information to answer specific questions. They will achieve some practice in looking for, accessing, and retrieving statistical information. This exercise can be done in class or as a homework assignment.

Tips for conducting the exercise: The sections can be broken into smaller assignments, depending on your need and time available. Check the websites before handing out the assignment to make sure that they are still active and the URLs are correct.

This exercise addresses ACRL Standard 2, Performance Indicators 3, 4, and 5.

Tools for Finding Statistics

One of the best places to start when you're looking for statistics is the *Statistical Abstract of the United States*, published annually since 1879 by the U.S. government.

In addition to providing statistics on a wide variety of subjects, the *Statistical Abstract* can also lead you to other statistics sources. At the bottom of each statistical table in the *Statistical Abstract*, you will find a reference to the original sources of these statistics. By consulting the original source, you may find additional statistical information on that topic. For example, the *Statistical Abstract* has statistics on the number of CDs teenagers buy. At the bottom of the table containing those statistics, the Recording Industry Association of America Inc. is listed as the source for the numbers. By going to the Recording Industry Association of America Inc. website, or by contacting this organization, it is likely that one could find additional statistics about the same topic. At the end of each edition of the *Statistical Abstract of the United States*, all the sources used for the statistical tables are listed. Keep in mind that each state has its own statistical abstract as well. The websites and addresses are listed in this section of the *Statistical Abstract of the United States*.

USING THE *STATISTICAL ABSTRACT OF THE UNITED STATES*

The United States government is one of the largest collectors of statistics in the world. The *Statistical Abstract of the United States* presents statistics on many different topics from many different sources.

Exercise 47

Statistics, Statistics, Statistics

Using the National Restaurant Association website, www.restaurant.org, answer the following questions:

> What were the total sales for U.S. restaurants in 2009? In 2000?
>
> How many restaurant jobs are there in Rhode Island?
>
> How many jobs is the restaurant industry expected to add in the next decade?
>
> How many eating and drinking places were there in Rhode Island in 2007?
>
> What information is *not* freely available to nonmembers?

To answer the following questions, access the Kids Count website, at www.aecf.org/kidscount/. From this address, click on Kids Count Databook Online.

> How many children are there in the United States under the age of eighteen?
>
> How many high school dropouts were counted for the most current year in the United States?
>
> What state had the highest percentage of high school dropouts in the latest year reported?
>
> Create a line graph for the percentage of families with children headed by a single parent. Select Connecticut, Massachusetts, and Rhode Island as your geographic region. Select the time period that covers the most current five years. Print your graph and attach. Which state has the highest percentage of single-parent households?
>
> Create a map for infant mortality rates for 2008. Name three states with a ranking more than 20 percent better than the median for all states.

Goal: Exercise 48 will familiarize students with the *Statistical Abstract of the United States* and the wide variety of statistics that are collected each year. It will also help them identify other sources of statistics that the government uses.

Description: For this exercise, students should use the most current year of the *Statistical Abstract of the United States.* The paper version seems to be more helpful for new users of this tool, but using it can be difficult, as most libraries only have one or two copies available. The web version is more cumbersome to use, but it will serve more students at the same time.

Tips for conducting the exercise: Students may need some practice in using the electronic version, as it is a little more complicated than the paper.

This exercise addresses ACRL Standard 2, Performance Indicators 3, 4, and 5.

EVALUATING STATISTICAL INFORMATION

Being able to evaluate statistical information is important, as statistics can be manipulated to tell the story that the person using them wants to tell. We have all heard how it is possible to lie with statistics. However, evaluating statistical information can be a very difficult task, and in some cases, it is something that only experts or others with advanced knowledge of statistics know how to do. It requires an in-depth understanding of the data-gathering process and the mathematical techniques used to generate the statistics.

With common sense, however, anyone can learn to be wary and critical of the numbers found and can avoid being duped by statistics. Here are a few general points to keep in mind when working with statistical information.

Who collected the data? Do they have a particular interest in the results?

Do the statistics show any bias?

Are the data timely?

Is the coverage complete? What was the size of the sample for the study?

Has the data been repackaged?

Is the data from a primary source? If it is from a secondary source, has it been properly documented so that you can find the primary source?

Experts and organizations are frequently overlooked as sources of information. With the appropriate tools to identify the experts and the information that will allow students to contact those experts, a rich new field of possibilities for insight and information becomes available.

Statistics are part of our lives. Knowing how to find appropriate statistics can add a dimension to any research endeavor. With a little practice, a student can easily see that statistics can be collected and interpreted to show just about anything. Learning how to assess and evaluate a statistic and its veracity will serve students for the rest of their lives.

Exercise 48

Finding U.S. Government–Supplied Statistics

Using the *Statistical Abstract of the United States,* answer the following questions. Use the latest year reported for your answers, and list the table number where you found your answer.

It is a well-known fact within the music industry that the category of consumers spending the most money on CDs and tapes is teenagers. What percentage of all buyers of sound recordings are between the ages of fifteen and nineteen?

How many deaths in the United States were caused by major cardiovascular disease?

How many travelers from the United States visited South America?

How many overseas travelers visited California?

How many existing one-family houses were sold in the United States, and what was the median sales price?

What percentage of public schools have Internet access?

How much asparagus is commercially produced in the United States? What state is the leading producer?

How much asparagus is used per capita (per person) in the United States?

VISUAL LITERACY AND STATISTICS

Contributed by Peter J. Larsen

This section is based on a visual literacy and statistics session from a semester-long information literacy course. The session draws heavily on these books:

Huff, Darrell. *How to Lie with Statistics*. New York: Norton, 1954.

Tufte, Edward R. *Visual Explanations*. Cheshire, CT: Graphics, 1997.

Although they are not by any means the last words on the subject, they are excellent introductions to the topic and full of examples that can easily be adapted for classroom use.

Statistics and Visual Literacy Assignment

The visual presentation of statistics can make them seem to imply almost anything. The same statistic can be used to support both sides of an argument. The information-literate student should consider how the visual display of statistics can affect their interpretation.

Goal: In this exercise, students practice looking at statistics and visual literacy examples and evaluating the arguments presented.

Description: This exercise is usually delivered through PowerPoint and addresses statistics and how they are displayed. The statistics section begins with a brief discussion of absolutely essential statistical ideas (mean, median, and mode) in a *very* general way. This is not meant to be a statistics class, but some knowledge of these terms is critical to understanding any depiction of statistical data. For instructors unfamiliar with statistical terms, Huff's book (listed above), which is a basic statistics text, or even Wikipedia will provide enough information for the simple level of discussion required for this assignment. The visual display of information section follows, using examples of arguments and charts where the meaning is obscured by accidental or deliberate misuse of graphic conventions. The idea is to show that the central ideas that make statistics useful can be displayed well or poorly, and evaluating charts is a critical skill in a world dominated by "infotainment."

Tips for conducting the exercise: This exercise is geared for a fifty-minute session, more or less evenly divided between statistics and visual literacy. It could be expanded or contracted by increasing or decreasing the depth of the information, the number of examples, and the number of problems at the end, although it is a complex-enough topic that covering all the material in less than fifty minutes is difficult. It could be split up into two separate sections. An effective way to deliver the questions is to display a slide with a scenario or image for discussion; then ask students to write down their answer and/or reaction, ask for answers from the class, and discuss the answer with another slide.

The blog *Strange Maps* (http://strangemaps.word press.com) is an excellent source for images that can be used for scenarios and discussions. There are a wide range of statistics and economics blogs that can be mined for ideas, although these often have a specific political agenda.

This exercise addresses ACRL Standard 3, Performance Indicators 2 and 3.

Some Basic Statistics

Basic Terms

Consider the following numbers: 5, 5, 5, 5, 10, 10, 10, 10, 10, 10, 10, 10, 15, 15, 75

What's the mean? The mean is the average. Add up the numbers and divide by the number of numbers. The total is 205. There are 15 numbers. Divide 205 by 15. The mean is 13.7.

What's the median? The median is the number in the middle. Start at both ends of the list of numbers and find the number in the middle. In this case, the median is 10.

What's the mode? The mode is the number that appears most frequently. In our list of numbers there are four 5s, eight 10s, two 15s, and one 75. The mode is 10 because there are more 10s than anything else.

Now you try it for the following salaries (in $1000s):
25, 25, 25, 25, 25, 25, 25, 40, 40, 40, 40, 90, 90, 90, 250

What's the mean?

What's the median?

What's the mode?

When Numbers Are Displayed Graphically

What are the advantages and disadvantages of each of the following charts?

Do you think they reflect the same data? Is one more honest than another?

CHART 1

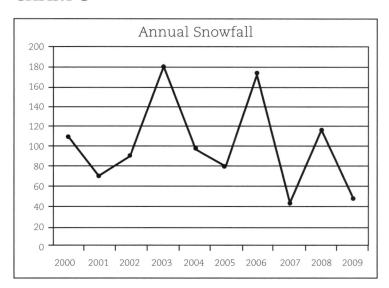

snowflake = 10 inches, rounded up

CHART 2

YEAR	CUMULATIVE SNOWFALL IN INCHES
2000	43
2001	29
2002	35
2003	71
2004	39
2005	31
2006	68
2007	18
2008	45
2009	20

CHART 3

Annual Snowfall

The three graphs all show a picture using the same data. What are some of the problems you see with the way each graph is created? Did you notice the lack of labels on the axes in chart 3? What are the most important things to think about when interpreting data provided visually?

Chapter Ten

The Paper Trail Project

COMPREHENSIVE ASSESSMENT: THE PAPER TRAIL PROJECT

The quest of many of today's students is to do their research fast! Very often this involves good intentions, the Internet, and, frequently, some cut-and-paste. These efforts do not always produce the results intended by the student and are generally unacceptable to the instructor or professor on the receiving end of the assignment. Information literacy projects, courses, and programs can help to alleviate this frustration by teaching students the best and most efficient tools and the techniques for using them.

At the University of Rhode Island, instructors use the semester-long Paper Trail Project as a vehicle for students to learn and apply information concepts and skills. These concepts and skills are experienced, practiced, learned, and applied by students in a number of smaller projects that culminate in the completion of the Paper Trail Project. This chapter will explain the goals of the project, the eight major parts of the project as they are explained to students, and our rationale for including each part in the project. We will also identify how each of the ACRL "Information Literacy Competency Standards for Higher Education, Standards, Performance Indicators, and Outcomes" applies to each part of the Paper Trail Project. A sample Paper Trail Project and a "Student Time Line for Completing the Paper Trail Project" are included as well, as is the rubric used to evaluate each student's project (see figure 10.1, "Grading Rubric for the Paper Trail Project").

Goals of the Paper Trail Project

The overall goal of the Paper Trail Project is for students to explore the information world by learning to use effective methods and techniques for gathering, evaluating, and presenting information. The knowledge gained from this project will prepare students to conduct university-level information research. The project requires students to learn and show expertise in all of the ACRL "Information Literacy

Competency Standards." By completing the Paper Trail Project, students will learn that quality research takes time, is rewarding, and can be done by beginning college and university students! Beyond this, the students' projects show evidence of their learning as indicated by the student-learning outcomes designed for the project. A rubric for the project will help you to determine how well the student(s) accomplished the project and how well the class as a whole has learned the information literacy concepts and skills.

Description

Simply described, the Paper Trail Project is an annotated, chronological "map" that follows the research journey for a research question of the student's design. The goal is to complete the research process and document it. Once completed, the eight parts of the project will accomplish the students' goals and the objectives of the Paper Trail Project. It is not necessary for students to actually write the research paper itself. If so desired, students could produce a brief report, a poster-presentation session, or a PowerPoint slide show as a way of sharing their answers to the research questions that they addressed; however, the main point here is that the research process is practiced and accomplished.

Paper Trail Project Student Learning Outcomes

There are eight major parts of the Paper Trail Project.
Part 1: Research Statement and Research Question. The research statement will include a single page with one or two paragraphs describing your topic, how and why you chose it, and the context within which you framed your research. Following that, state the research question that you developed for the Paper Trail project. Part 1 addresses ACRL Standard 1, Performance Indicator 1, learning outcomes a–f; Performance Indicator 2, learning outcomes a–d; Performance Indicator 4, learning outcomes a and b; and Standard 2, Performance Indicator 3, learning outcome b; Performance Indicator 4, learning outcomes b and c; Performance Indicator 5, learning outcome a.

Part 2: Table of Contents. A single page lists each section of the project in the order it appears in the Paper Trail. Part 2 addresses ACRL Standard 2, Performance Indicator 5, learning outcomes b and c; and Standard 5, Performance Indicator 2, learning outcome f; Performance Indicator 3, learning outcome a.

Part 3: Discovery and Planning. This section includes a variety of evidence that displays and illustrates how you developed your topic and research question. Include the concept map, encyclopedia citation, and annotation. For the encyclopedia article, include the citation and annotation for your useful encyclopedia article. As supporting documentation, also include physical evidence or access to the evidence of the encyclopedia title page and first page of the article. Part 3 addresses Standard 1, Performance Indicator 1, learning outcomes a and b; Standard 2, Performance Indicator 1, learning outcomes a–d; Performance Indicator 2, learning outcomes a–f; Performance Indicator 3, learning outcomes a–d; Performance Indicator 4, learning outcomes a–c; Performance Indicator 5, learning outcomes a–e; and Standard 4, Performance Indicator 1, learning outcomes a and b.

Part 4: Research Outline. In this section present an outline for your research question. It should include enough ideas and supporting sources to allow you to write an eight- to ten-page paper or to present a fifteen- to twenty-minute presentation. Your outline is the organizational plan of your research project. As part of the outline, indicate which source provided information for different points by including the author's name and year of the source. The outline demonstrates how you directed your research efforts in order to develop a thoughtful, in-depth answer to your research question. Part 4 addresses ACRL Standard 1, Performance Indicator 1, learning outcomes a–f; and Standard 2, Performance Indicator 1, learning outcomes c and d; Performance Indicator 2, learning outcomes a–f; Performance Indicator 3, learning outcome b.

Part 5A: Annotated Bibliography of Relevant and Useful Sources. In this section, compile all the sources you decided to use into one annotated bibliography. Sources should be listed alphabetically by author. Make all necessary corrections as noted in feedback provided in earlier drafts; the final bibliography should be free of any correction marks or notes.

Part 5B: Supporting Documentation for 5A. Follow the annotated bibliography with evidence of the supporting documents from your research, including photocopies, printouts, articles, book title pages, etc. Be sure to organize the sources to match the bibliography's order—alphabetically by author's name.

Part 6A: Annotated Bibliography of Less-Relevant and Not-Useful Sources. Compile all the sources you decided not to use into a second annotated bibliography. Sources should be listed alphabetically by author. Make all necessary corrections as noted in prior feedback. The final bibliography should be free of any correction marks or notes.

Part 6B: Supporting Documentation for 6A. Follow this annotated bibliography section with evidence of the supporting documents from your research, including photocopies, printouts, articles, book title pages, etc. Be sure to organize the sources so they match the bibliography's order—alphabetically by author's name.

Parts 5 and 6 address ACRL Standard 2, Performance Indicator 1, learning outcomes c and d; Performance Indicator 2, learning outcomes a–f; Performance Indicator 3, learning outcomes a–c; Performance Indicator 4, learning outcomes a–c; Performance Indicator 5, learning outcomes a–c; Standard 3, Performance Indicator 1, learning outcome a; Performance Indicator 2, learning outcomes a–d; Performance Indicator 4, learning outcomes a, b, c, and e; Standard 4, Performance Indicator 1, learning outcomes a and b; Performance Indicator 2, learning outcomes a and b; Performance Indicator 3, learning outcomes a and b; Standard 5, Performance Indicator 1, learning outcome d; Performance Indicator 2, learning outcomes a–f; Performance Indicator 3, learning outcomes a and b.

Part 7: Research Journal. In this section, include all of your individual research journal entries. All required entries should be included. Each entry is thorough and addresses the required issues. Organize in chronological order, first to last, over the length of the project. Part 7 addresses ACRL Standard 2, Performance Indicator 1, learning outcomes a–d; Standard 3, Performance Indicator 2, learning outcomes a–d; Standard 4, Performance Indicator 2, learning outcomes a and b; Performance Indicator 3, learning outcomes a and d; and Standard 5, Performance Indicator 1, learning outcomes b and d; Performance Indicator 2, learning outcome f.

Part 8: Research Summary. Use the "Research Summary Guidelines" and develop a thoughtful essay on your semester's work. Your "Research Summary" should be a thorough, thoughtful reflection of the research process, successes and challenges, usefulness, and final outcomes. You should also consider how this project has contributed to your development as an information-literate person. Part 8 addresses ACRL Standard 1, Performance Indicator 1, learning outcomes a–f; Performance Indicator 2, learning outcomes a–f; Performance Indicator 3, learning outcomes a–c; Performance Indicator 4, learning outcomes a and b; Standard 2, Performance Indicator 1, learning outcomes c and d; Performance Indicator 2,

learning outcome a; Performance Indicator 4, learning outcomes a–c; Performance Indicator 5, learning outcomes c–e; Standard 3, Performance Indicator 2, learning outcomes a–d; Performance Indicator 4, learning outcomes a–e; Performance Indicator 5, learning outcomes a and b; Performance Indicator 6, learning outcomes a–c; Standard 4, Performance Indicator 1, learning outcome b; Performance Indicator 2, learning outcomes a and b; Performance Indicator 3, learning outcomes a–d; and Standard 5, Performance Indicator 1, learning outcomes a–d; Performance Indicator 2, learning outcomes a–g; Performance Indicator 3, learning outcomes a and b.

Explaining the Parts of the Paper Trail Project

Part 1: Research Statement and Research Question. Students are told they will be doing a semester-long research project that asks them to focus on the process of finding, evaluating, and using information. They may choose any topic of interest to them. The instructor may suggest that students look to their program of studies or specific courses they are enrolled in at college, topics that they are passionate about but have not yet researched academically, or a current trend or news item that interests them. Tell the students that they will do several exercises and assignments to help them develop a research statement that describes their topic and explains why they chose the topic as well as defining a context for their research topic. Using the ideas generated from the exercises and assignments, they will design a research question to use for the project duration.

Part 2: Table of Contents. Requiring students to develop a table of contents for the Paper Trail helps students to organize all the parts, prevents students from overlooking specific parts of the project, and provides a path for the instructor to follow the student's work.

Part 3: Discovery and Planning. Provide activities that help students consider and expand their ideas on the topic they have chosen with the goal of developing a research question. Focusing and refining can be achieved through the brainstorming process of concept mapping. Concept mapping is a familiar brainstorming tool, and it can be done using either paper and pencil or using free or commercial software programs, such as bubbl.us (http://bubbl.us) or Inspiration software. Using the ideas generated from exercise 12, "Create a Concept Map," students should develop an open-ended research question that allows them to solve a problem or take a stand on an issue.

Part 4: Research Outline. The outline is the organizational plan of the research project. Using the concept map and the research question, as well as the selected sources gathered over the semester, students develop an outline that reflects the investigation of the topic. For each heading and subheading of the outline, students should indicate which source provided information for different points by including the author's name and year of the source. The completed outline demonstrates how the student directed his or her research efforts in order to develop a thoughtful response to the research question.

Part 5A: Annotated Bibliography of Relevant and Useful Sources. The bibliography illustrates the student's ability to find, evaluate, and use information sources effectively. Over a period of fourteen to sixteen weeks, each student will create mini bibliographies of books, articles, and websites. This final annotated bibliography requires students to reevaluate all of the sources gathered one last time and to select ten (of those fifteen) very best sources that answer the research question. The bibliography will include an alphabetical list of these ten sources, cited appropriately. Each source annotation will include both a brief description and an evaluation based on criteria. The annotation will also explain how the source is relevant to the research question. Students need to describe what part of the research question each selected source addresses.

Part 5B: Supporting Documentation for 5A. This part of the project is twofold. For the student, it teaches the importance of keeping a log or file of sources of all the research done from the preliminary foray to the final stages of answering his or her research question. For the instructor, seeing the actual sources proves fairly well that students have not simply cut and pasted or plagiarized another's research into their own. All the source documentation must match the sources submitted in the bibliography. This is not easy to accomplish unless the student has actually done the research with some degree of integrity. Documentation can be provided as photocopies, printouts, or electronically, using Digital Object Identifier (DOI) numbers, PURLs (Persistent URLs), and URLs.

Part 6A: Annotated Bibliography of Less-Relevant and Not-Useful Sources. This bibliography emphasizes the student's skill in recognizing a source's faults or lack of relevance for a particular research question.

This is one of the more difficult tasks for students after they have committed to fifteen sources that seem to meet their needs. The effort expended in fine-tuning their choices helps students understand that not every good source is the "right" source.

Part 6B: Supporting Documentation for 6A. See directly above, "Part 5B."

Part 7: Research Journal. The research journal provides a means for students to reflect on the total research process. In journal entries students should discuss how they went about finding a resource and how easy or difficult the search was. Ask students to think about how the resources they found did or did not answer their research question. Suggest they consider writing about the search planning, search implementation, source discovery and evaluation, and, finally, citing and annotating the materials they have selected.

Some students are more comfortable than others sharing personal thoughts and feelings in written form, so the range of reflection will vary. Experience has shown that students who find it difficult to put their experiences in writing will eventually visit the instructor for some help and guidance. After the discussion, the instructor might say, "OK, right now, write down some notes about this visit with me as one of your journal entries. What happened here? Can you describe how you feel about the project, about the sources you are finding or not finding? What decisions did you make about the research?" Explain that these are the kinds of comments the instructor expects to see in the journal entries for the project.

Some students will discover that they enjoy the challenge of academic research. Others will hate the amount of effort and time necessary to find their research sources. Some may simply provide declarative statements in their journals with no hint of the personal experiential journey. Encourage students to share their trials and tribulations. Be firm in your expectations for the research journal. The journaling process allows students to articulate their research needs in an informal, reflective manner. Writing entries in research journals helps students develop their ideas along the paper trail. The process of writing journal entries crystallizes the research process.

Part 8: Research Summary. The research summary tells the journey each student took doing his or her Paper Trail Project. There are two parts to the summary. Students use the following questions to reflect on the accomplishments and challenges of the research process.

1. Information need. Did you find enough information to enable you to answer your research question?

   - Are there any gaps or missing pieces that you would prefer to have before developing the answer?

   - Can you describe what is missing? ("I would have liked to have found . . .")

2. Information literacy. Think back over the course and answer these questions within your essay:

   - How did the research process go overall?

   - What was the hardest part? What was the easiest part?

   - For your research need, what were the best sources?

   - Did you have an "aha" moment in thinking about information and doing research in this course?

   - Have you changed anything about the way you search, evaluate, and use information outside of academics?

   - Finally, pass along one piece of advice about information research to a non–Library 120 student.

Methods of Facilitating the Project

The Paper Trail Project can be approached in several ways. Our experience is using it in an information literacy credit course, but it could easily be used within a subject-specific course that has an integrated information literacy program.

Using the exercises provided in this book, class time can be used to demonstrate, experience, and practice information literacy concepts involved in completing the Paper Trail Project. This project is based on the time allowed for a fourteen- to sixteen-week, three-credit course. When time is limited, the actual number of required sources for each of the bibliographies in the project may be reduced.

The Paper Trail Project can be completed by individual students or by small groups of students. For a group project, the instructor could ask the students to develop a research question using a starting point such as environmental issues or other current topics of global or national concern. If the small-group method is chosen, be sure to create individual tasks within the group so that each student can be assessed individually. For example,

the group can work together to design the research question. Individual students can contribute work on different aspects of the research, and together the group will make decisions on sources to include. Individual students can write the research journal entries for the parts of the research that they themselves worked on, or the group might create a journal entry together, depending on the approach the teacher has chosen.

In the optimal situation, students will be allowed as much time as possible to practice their information literacy skills by doing exercises or homework assignments that prepare them to complete all of the project parts. Instructors should set due dates for each part or section of the Paper Trail Project. This will help students manage their time and allow plenty of time for revision after students have received your feedback.

Introducing the Paper Trail Project

Introduce this project early and refresh students' memories often.

Explain to students that the project is based primarily on the goals and objectives of being information-literate students: their ability to gather, evaluate, and effectively use the resources they provide in their projects. This project is both the documentation and the personal journey of a student through the experience of the research process. Students should be told that the process will be messy. This is expected and accepted because it reflects the true nature of research. The Paper Trail Project is a great opportunity for students to try methods out over a period of time—be it only a few weeks or an entire semester—often without the added pressures of having to complete the paper or project for a subject-based course.

Students may be overwhelmed with the immensity of the project. Explain that it will be done step-by-step with the instructor guiding and facilitating the class. The class members will act as an informal support group as they progress through the assignments that lead up to the finished Paper Trail Project. In the end, most students are amazed by the amount of information they have gathered and the quality of the resources they have amassed for this project.

Students consider it strange to document the research process and not write the paper. Do all in your power to be clear that the *process* is the project, not the final paper!

Project Presentation Formats

The Paper Trail Project is specifically designed without a prescribed presentation style or format parameters. There are many required components, but the manner in which students choose to present their project is purposely left open. The project should be clearly outlined and firm in its expectations while at the same time flexible enough to allow variations in format.

Examples of Paper Trail presentations include the old reliable three-ring binder with page separators, or the more contemporary presentation styles: web pages, blogs, wiki, Google-doc, PowerPoint presentations, and videos. Of course, there are time limitations, and these must be considered by the instructor when contemplating various formats. Allowing flexibility in presentation format leaves room for creativity and for accommodation of multiple learning styles.

Tips for Guiding Students through the Project

The Paper Trail Project is meant to teach students effective and reliable methods to use as they proceed through college-level research. At the same time, it exposes the side trips that occur while one is involved in research. A benefit of the Paper Trail Project is that instructors can easily intervene to help students stay on track and remain successful. Instructors can help students during the semester by guiding their progress toward completion of this project. Here is a list of possible suggestions to follow:

On quizzes and tests, include an extra-credit question that might ask students to describe the point they have reached in researching their Paper Trail Project or tell how they are feeling about the research process and the Paper Trail Project.

Choose specific colors or type or design a symbol to brand the Paper Trail exercises and assignments that are part of the Paper Trail. Whether you are working in print or online, there are many ways to mark the documents so students will be alerted to their relevance and importance to the project.

Remind students of your office hours, send out e-mail alert notices, and mention the project in class.

At midsemester, and again closer toward the end of the project (adjust according to your time frame), hold an outside-of-class workshop for students who want to bring in their "stuff" for advice and help.

Require that each student schedule a brief in-person meeting with you to discuss their progress. You can make this graded or nongraded, but usually "mandatory" is enough to get them to come visit you.

Provide several examples of past Paper Trail Projects and bring these to the classroom, put them on reserve in your library, or keep them available in your office. (Note: be sure to get student authors' permission before you do this.)

The project design generally protects students from mediocrity or failure. However, instructors should be prepared for last-minute realizations such as "I just realized I've been heading in the wrong direction for weeks!" "I just found a gold mine in a slightly different vein," or "This topic is killing me, and I really need help!" These are natural occurrences, and this project encourages them to be seen as part of the learning experience.

A class web page, a class discussion list, personal consultations, and individual e-mails can all be used to support students while they travel the paper trail. There are students who will appear to breeze through the project, and for them the project is good practice for learning college-level research tools. There are also students who may not seem to have the "can-do" attitude or the creativity to complete this project. Perhaps these are the students who benefit most from the structure and support of the Paper Trail Project. Information literacy, a goal for lifelong learners and considered an important part of the college skill set by many, is worth a little cheerleading!

Grading Criteria for the Paper Trail Project

If used as the culminating project for a subject course (such as history or nursing) or for an information literacy credit course, this project should be weighted heavily. The rubric in figure 10.1 gives an example of a grading scheme. Keen attention to each part is necessary for successful completion of the project. Should a student overlook or skim lightly the work required for even one section, it will seriously impact the total work of the project. Provide a copy of the rubric for the students so they are clear as to what the expectations are and how they may attain the grade they desire.

Tips on Using the Grading Criteria

The clear grading criteria in the rubric enable both the students and the instructor to understand exactly what has been agreed on for the project requirements. Share the expected student learning outcomes with students

The Paper Trail Project

What Is a Paper Trail?

The *Encarta World English Dictionary* (2009) defines a paper trail as a "sequence of documents that can be used by an investigator as a record of someone's actions or decisions." Investigators examining the 2001 financial collapse of the energy corporation Enron pursued a paper trail that eventually led to criminal charges and convictions against several Enron officials.

Here, however, you are the researcher-investigator pursuing information that is relevant to your research question. You are also the author of your own paper trail—an annotated, chronological record of your research efforts and overall outcome.

Use this guide to ensure that your project is complete and organized before handing it in.

What should the Paper Trail include?

	ITEM	DETAILS
1.	Research Statement and Research Question	A single page with one or two paragraphs describing your topic, how/why you chose it, and the context within which you framed your research. State your research question below your research statement.
2.	Table of Contents for your Paper Trail	A single page that lists your sections in the order they appear in the Paper Trail.
3.	Research Outline—one that would assist you in writing an eight- to ten-page paper	MANDATORY: Projects submitted without an outline cannot be graded. Your outline is the organizational plan of your research paper. As part of the outline, indicate which source provided information for different points by including the author's name and year of the source (see example). The outline demonstrates how you directed your research efforts in order to develop a thoughtful, in-depth answer to your research question.
4.	Background Information Encyclopedia Assignment	Citation and annotation for your useful encyclopedia article. Concept map. Supporting documentation—photocopies of encyclopedia title page and first page of article.
5a.	Annotated Bibliography of Relevant and Useful Sources	Compile all the sources you decided to use into one annotated bibliography. Sources should be listed alphabetically by author. Make all necessary corrections as noted; the final bibliography should be free of any correction marks or notes.
5b.	Supporting Documentation (for above sources)	Follow the annotated bibliography section with the supporting documents from your research, including photocopies, printouts, articles, book title pages, etc. Organize to match the bibliography's order—alphabetically by author's name.

(cont.)

	ITEM	DETAILS
6a.	Annotated Bibliography of Less-Relevant and Not-Useful Sources	Compile all the sources you decided not to use into a second annotated bibliography. Sources should be listed alphabetically by author/main entry. Make all necessary corrections as noted; final bibliography should be free of any correction marks or notes.
6b.	Supporting Documentation (for above sources)	Follow the annotated bibliography section with the supporting documents from your research, including photocopies, printouts, articles, book title pages, etc. Organize to match the bibliography's order—alphabetically by author's name.
7.	Research Journal	Provide all of your individual research journal entries. Make any required corrections before including. Entries with comments but no required corrections may be included "as is." Organize in chronological order, first to last, and be sure your name is on each one.
8.	Research Summary	A thoughtful essay on your semester's work. See "Research Summary Guidelines."

What is *not* included in the Paper Trail?

Any worksheets, tables, etc., that you completed as part of the assignments

Any handouts, exercises, etc., that you did in class

Any uncorrected required components

Your semester project *must* be well organized. I should be able to examine it without becoming confused about what is what and where it is. Use a three-ring binder and tabs.

Research Summary Guidelines

Your research summary is a thoughtful essay on your semester's work. You may prefer to divide it into two parts as described. Please type it, double-spaced, with a 10- or 12-point font.

Part 1: Research statement and research question

Did you find enough information to enable you to answer your research question?
Are there any gaps or missing pieces that you would prefer to have before developing the answer?
Can you describe what is missing? ("I would have liked to have found . . .")

Part 2: Information literacy. Think back over the course and answer these questions within your essay:

How did the research process go overall?
What was the hardest part? What was the easiest part?
For your research need, what were the best sources?
Did you have an "aha" moment in thinking about information and doing research in this course?
Have you changed anything about the way you search, evaluate, and use information outside of academics?
Finally, pass along one piece of advice about information research to a non–Library 120 student.

Figure 10.1

GRADING RUBRIC FOR THE PAPER TRAIL PROJECT

ELEMENT	EXCEEDS ALL EXPECTATIONS	MEETS EXPECTATIONS	DOES NOT MEET EXPECTATIONS	FAILS TO MEET EXPECTATIONS	SCORE
Project Organization	5 Table of contents clear and accurate. Paper Trail organized as required and clearly labeled.	4 Table of contents mostly clear and accurate; most items in order and clearly labeled.	3 Table of contents marginally adequate; some items out of order or not clearly labeled.	2–0 Table of contents insufficient; numerous items out of order or not clearly labeled.	
Defining, Planning, and Refining	5 Includes a variety of supporting evidence displaying an evolving, reflective research process. Includes encyclopedia research, concept mapping, and drafts/revisions of research statements.	4 Includes several meaningful pieces of supporting evidence displaying an evolving, reflective research process.	3 Includes some meaningful supporting evidence of an evolving, reflective research process.	2–0 Includes some supporting evidence of the research process but may not demonstrate meaningful progress or reflection.	
Research Statement and Question	5 Topic is academically oriented, has depth. Statement and question are clear, with a compelling rationale.	4 Topic is academically oriented, has some depth. Statement and question are identifiable, with good research rationale.	3 Topic is vaguely stated and may not be academically oriented. Some rationale for statement/question is provided but may be unclear.	2–0 Topic is barely described, is not academically oriented, and/or lacks depth. No rationale for statement/question is evident.	

(cont.)

Figure 10.1 (cont.)

ELEMENT	EXCEEDS ALL EXPECTATIONS	MEETS EXPECTATIONS	DOES NOT MEET EXPECTATIONS	FAILS TO MEET EXPECTATIONS	SCORE
Outline	10–9 Outline sufficient to organize an 8- to 10-page paper. Includes relevant source citations.	8–7 Mostly sufficient to organize a major research paper; contains most relevant source citations.	6–5 Included, but not substantive enough for a major research paper. May contain only a few source citations.	4–0 Incomplete or insufficient; does not contain relevant source citations.	
Bibliography: Sources	20–17 All 15 sources included meet project criteria for type, quality, and variety. Contains at least 15 useful sources.	16–13 Most sources meet criteria for type, quality, and variety. At least 9 of 15 included sources are useful.	12–9 Over half the sources included meet criteria for type, quality, and variety. At least 8 useful sources for a total of 12.	8–0 Half or fewer of the included sources meet criteria for type, quality, variety, and usefulness.	
Bibliography: Citations	10–9 All citations are in the assigned citation style.	8–7 At least 12 citations are in assigned style, or 1 element is missing in all citations.	6–5 At least 9 citations are in assigned style, or 2 elements are missing in all citations.	4–0 8 or fewer citations are in assigned style, or 3 elements are missing in all citations.	
Bibliography: Annotations	20–17 All annotations evaluate source content, author credibility, and relevance.	16–13 At least 12 annotations evaluate source content, author credibility, and relevance.	12–9 At least 9 annotations evaluate source content, author credibility, and relevance.	8–0 8 or fewer annotations evaluate source content, author credibility, and relevance.	
Bibliography: Supporting Materials	10–9 All supporting materials included. All materials organized as required and clearly labeled.	8–7 Materials for at least 12 sources included. Organized and clearly labeled.	6–5 Materials for at least 9 sources included. Organized and labeled.	4–0 Materials for 8 or fewer sources included. May not be organized and labeled.	

ELEMENT	EXCEEDS ALL EXPECTATIONS	MEETS EXPECTATIONS	DOES NOT MEET EXPECTATIONS	FAILS TO MEET EXPECTATIONS	SCORE
Research Logs	5 All required entries included. Each entry is thorough and addresses the required issues.	4 All required entries included. Most are thorough and address the required issues.	3 One or two research logs are missing or do not fully address the required issues.	2–0 More than two research logs missing or do not address the required issues.	
Research Summary	10–9 Thorough, thoughtful reflection on the research process, successes and challenges, usefulness, and final outcomes.	8–7 Mostly thorough reflection on the research process. Addresses most of the required elements.	6–5 Considers most required elements but lacks sufficient thoroughness or reflection.	4–0 Lacks discussion on most of the required elements; may summarize but lacks reflection.	

On time?   YES   NO
If no, number of days late: _____ x 10 = _____
(Late penalty to be subtracted from total)

as they move from part to part in the research experience. Explain what the project must include to be successful in fulfilling the eight different parts. As stated in the beginning of this chapter, the overall goal of the project is not simply a grade but for students to learn to understand information concepts and to explore the information world through gathering, evaluating, and presenting information. Keeping that in mind, what is most important to the grade? The overall integrity and quality of the research are the most important attributes to look for when grading. Grading Paper Trail Projects must be done based on the integrity of the student's process and the quality of the sources discovered, but not on whether the research question was perfectly or completely answered. Many students

falsely believe that they should be able to solve all of their academic questions and completely answer all of the research issues they address. Allowing students to focus on the research process and select the best evidence they can find will produce students who can pursue high-quality research and researchers who will stay lifelong learners.

Assessing the Project

If used as the culminating project for a credit course, we recommend a very high weighted grade of 25 to 30 percent. Remind students that the grade is based on a series of assignments that they will have already had ample opportunity to practice and revise.

Example of a Completed Paper Trail Project

Student author: Samantha Cummings

Topic: Sex Trafficking
Research Statement

The issue of sex trafficking is one that I had heard little about while I was growing up. In recent years, however, I have noticed the issue being discussed more and more in the media. From television programs such as *Law and Order,* to news coverage, to campus forums, and most recently the popular movie *Taken,* sex trafficking is beginning to gain recognition as a serious threat to the safety and well-being of many women and children. It was from these media that I first began to take an interest in the issue of sex trafficking. I was particularly moved to learn more about the issue after discovering that Providence, Rhode Island, a city not far from my residence, has high instances of trafficked women and children as it is the only state (aside from certain counties in Nevada) in which indoor prostitution is still legal.

For these reasons, I chose to conduct my research project on sex trafficking. I was most interested to learn about the victims of sex trafficking, particularly who they are and how they became victims. I feel that the first step to preventing future instances of sex trafficking is to recognize the victims and understand how they became involved in the sex trade. As knowledge is power, if more people were aware of how victims become involved in the sex trade then they could perhaps avoid becoming victims themselves. I was able to use these ideas to formulate a focused research question.

Research Question: Who are the victims of sex trafficking, and how do they become victims?

Table of Contents

Research Paper Outline: Sex Trafficking

I. Introduction
   A. Summary of the topic
   B. Definition of sex trafficking—*New Internationalist,* 2007
   C. Distinction between sex trafficking and prostitution—Batsyukova, 2007

II. Overview
   A. Brief history of sex trafficking—Cree, 2008
   B. How the sex trafficking industry operates—Bhattacharyya, 2005
   C. Facts and figures—*New Internationalist,* 2007

III. Victims
   A. Victim testimony—Sorajjakool, 2003, and Polaris Project, 2009
   B. Who they are—Feingold, 2005
   C. How they become victims—Shelley, 2003—
   D. What happens to trafficked victims—*New Internationalist,* 2007
   E. Sex trafficking in different regions—Bolder Image, 2009

IV. Prevention
   A. Raising awareness—SwirlyGig Media, 2005
   B. Reducing demand—Yen, 2008
   C. Government action—Academy for Educational Development, 2008

V. Restoration
   A. Civil rights of victims—Nam, 2007
   B. Community outreach—Bolder Image, 2009
   C. Report trafficking—Polaris Project, 2009

VI. Conclusion

Encyclopedia Assignment

Maddex, Robert L. "Human Trafficking." *Encyclopedia of Sexual Behavior and the Law.* District of Columbia: CQ Press, 2006.

The article "Human Trafficking," by Robert L. Maddex, begins by giving a brief history of the trafficking of humans, particularly in the area of sex trafficking. The article goes on to discuss the magnitude of the problem, citing the increase of trafficking in places like Eastern Europe and even the United States, noting that the majority of the victims of sex trafficking are female immigrants. The article provides examples of a number of U.S. federal laws, such as the Victims of Trafficking and Violence Protection Act, that outlaw the trafficking of humans for sexual or immoral purposes. It also provides a brief history of the amendments and evolutions of such laws making them more specific and including harsher penalties for offenders. The article, however, states that there was a lack of enforcement for such laws, as well as a number of other drawbacks, including immigrant women falsifying claims in order to stay in the country. However, it goes on to state that a number of changes and improvements have been made to the Victims of Trafficking and Violence Protection Act and cites two court cases that are proof that trafficking will be prosecuted and trafficking laws will be upheld.

Annotated Bibliography of Relevant Sources

Academy for Educational Development. *A Web Resource For Combating Human Trafficking.* 2008. Academy for Educational Development. 13 April 2009 (www .humantrafficking.org).

This website serves to unite government and non-government organizations in the East Asia and Pacific regions in the fights against human trafficking. The website does so by providing information specific to countries in these regions including action plans, national laws, and contact information for government agencies and NGOs in each individual country. It also provides website viewers with information regarding the prevention of trafficking, rehabilitation and protection for victims, and initiatives on the local and global scale. It is in this section that I was able to find information most relevant to my research topic. On the page titled "Prevention," I found useful information detailing the causes of trafficking and the tactics some criminal groups use to coerce victims into the sex trade industry, answering the part of my research question concerning how victims become involved in sex trafficking. I believe this website meets the evaluation criteria for a number of reasons, including that it is supported by the U.S. Department of State, references and cites other credible sources, and is well maintained, timely, and professional.

Batsyukova, Svitlana. "Prostitution and Human Trafficking for Sexual Exploitation." *Gender Issues* 24.2 (June 2007): 46–50. Academic Search Premier. EBSCO. University of Rhode Island. University Library, Kingston, RI. 25 Feb. 2009. http://0-search.ebscohost .com.helin.uri.edu/login.aspx?direct=true&db=aph& AN=27053621&site=ehost-live.

This article explores sex trafficking as one of the most prevalent reasons for human trafficking as well as outlines the differences between sex trafficking and prostitution. The article argues that sex trafficking is in fact the exploitation of prostitution. In addition, the article looks at the policies for and against prostitution. This article is relevant to my research because it will help me to understand who the victims of sex trafficking are as well as the core differences between sex trafficking and prostitution. For instance, the article will help me to determine whether those men and women who voluntarily participate in acts of prostitution can be considered victims like those who are exploited. Author Svitlana Batsyukova has earned her master's degree from the University of Washington in public administration. I narrowed my search results on Academic Search Premier to search specifically for scholarly peer-reviewed journals, so the journal from which this article originated should be a scholarly journal.

Bhattacharyya, Gargi. *Traffick: The Illicit Movement of People and Things.* London; Ann Arbor: Pluto Press, 2005.

Traffick: The Illicit Movement of People and Things explores the illegal economy of trafficking such commodities as drugs, money, arms, and people. Author Gargi Bhattacharyya argues that the illegal world of trafficking allows for global expansion and is depended upon by the official economy for cheap labor, finance, and access to new markets. *Traffick* explores the mechanics of this illegal economy, specifically examining, in four sections, drugs, arms, organized crime, and the trafficking of humans. It looks to the past for explanations for this illegal market as well as explores what the future may hold. Author Gargi Bhattacharyya is a professor of cultural politics

CONCEPT MAP FOR SEX TRAFFICKING

Example of a completed Paper Trail Project.

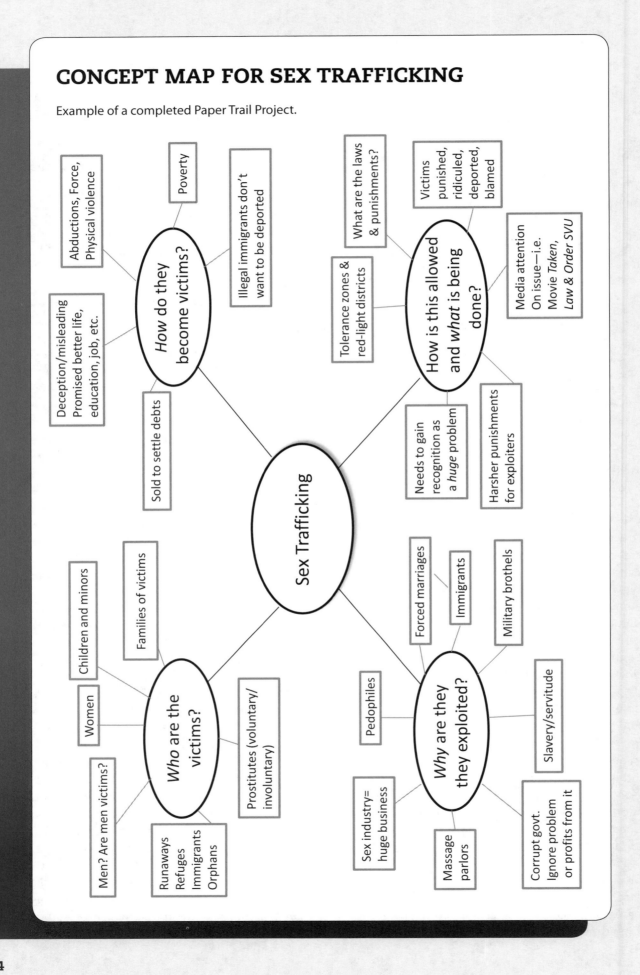

Sex Trafficking

How do they become victims?
- Poverty
- Abductions, Force, Physical violence
- Illegal immigrants don't want to be deported
- Deception/misleading Promised better life, education, job, etc.
- Sold to settle debts

How is this allowed and what is being done?
- What are the laws & punishments?
- Victims punished, ridiculed, deported, blamed
- Media attention On issue—i.e. Movie *Taken*, *Law & Order SVU*
- Tolerance zones & red-light districts
- Needs to gain recognition as a *huge* problem
- Harsher punishments for exploiters

Who are the victims?
- Children and minors
- Families of victims
- Women
- Men? Are men victims?
- Runaways Refuges Immigrants Orphans
- Prostitutes (voluntary/involuntary)

Why are they exploited?
- Forced marriages
- Immigrants
- Military brothels
- Pedophiles
- Slavery/servitude
- Sex industry= huge business
- Massage parlors
- Corrupt govt. Ignore problem or profits from it

and religion at the University of Birmingham. She is also the author of two other books on her specialty. Sections of this book will be relevant to my research on sex trafficking, specifically the section on trafficking of humans. The book in its entirety, however, is helpful in allowing me to better understand the mechanics of the trafficking market and how and why trafficking is allowed to exist. The author appears to be credible and accurate, as does the information the book contains. *Traffick* was published in 2005, so the information is still fairly current and reliable, and the back of the book contains an extensive bibliography of sources.

Bolder Image. *Shared Hope International.* 2009. Shared Hope International. 13 April 2009. www.sharedhope .org/index.asp.

This website serves as the official website for Shared Hope International, a nonprofit organization formed by former congresswoman Linda Smith. The organization and website are dedicated to rescuing and restoring trafficked women and children as well as preventing and eliminating sex trafficking across the globe. The website provides facts and information on sex trafficking, opportunities for visitors to the website to help victims by donating and volunteering, and a comprehensive overview of the actions and steps being taken by Shared Hope International, including a map of different regions that the organization has helped. The latter is the most relevant to answering my research question as it allows me to use the interactive map to see what countries victims come from and how they become victims under different circumstances in different regions. The website appears to be well maintained and frequently updated, and it is run by a credible nonprofit organization.

Cree, Viviene E. "Confronting Sex Trafficking: Lessons from History." *International Social Work* 51.6 (2008) 763–776. Social Services Abstracts (CSA). U of Rhode Island Lib. 23 March 2009. http://0-csaweb109v.csa .com/helin.uri.edu.

This article explores the problem of sex trafficking, including how widespread of an issue it is and what can be done in response to the problem. This article explores victims of sex trafficking worldwide and will help me answer the question "Who are the victims and how do they become victims?" For this reason, this article is relevant to my research. This article is found in the journal *International Social Work*. The website for the journal states that it is a scholarly/peer-reviewed

publication. The article also cites many sources and is very current. The author of this article is a professor of social work at the University of Edinburgh.

Feingold, David A. "Human Trafficking." *Foreign Policy* (Sept. 2005): 26–32. Academic Search Premier. EBSCO. University of Rhode Island. University Library, Kingston, RI. 25 Feb. 2009. http://0-search.ebscohost .com.helin.uri.edu/login.aspx?direct=true&db=aph& AN=17981371&site=ehost-live.

This article explores the various forms of human trafficking, including but not limited to the trafficking of men, women, and children for use in the sex trade. It also looks closely at whether certain laws such as anti-immigration laws and the legalization of prostitution will increase or decrease instances of sex trafficking. This article is relevant to my research because it will explore the second part of my research question ("How do the victims of sex trafficking become victims?") as this article looks at the effects laws have on the sex trade industry. Author David A. Feingold is the international coordinator for HIV/AIDS and trafficking projects for UNESCO as well as the director of the Ophidian Research Institute. I also found this article using Academic Search Premier and limiting my search results to scholarly journals.

Nam, Jennifer S. "The Case of the Missing Case: Examining the Civil Right of Action for Human Trafficking Victims." *Columbia Law Review* 107.7 (Nov. 2007): 1655–1703. Academic Search Premier. EBSCO. University of Rhode Island. University Library, Kingston, RI. 24 Feb. 2009. http://0-search.ebscohost .com.helin.uri.edu/login.aspx?direct=true&db=aph& AN=27551529&site=ehost-live.

This article examines the civil rights afforded the victims of sex trafficking under the Trafficking Victims Protection Reauthorization Act of 2003. It also makes a number of policy recommendations with the hopes that they will encourage more victims to come forward in the future. As my research topic focuses on the victims of sex trafficking, this article is relevant to my research as it discusses legal options that are available to the victims. This article does not provide background information on the author; however, the journal, *Columbia Law Review,* is a scholarly journal. From reviewing the journal online, it appears to be a reputable journal. The website for the *Columbia Law Review* claims to be one of the leading publications of legal scholarship and states that it is published entirely by students at Columbia Law School.

New Internationalist. "Sex Trafficking: The Facts." *New Internationalist* 1.404 (2007): 1–3. Women's Studies International. University of Rhode Island. University Library, Kingston, RI. 23 March 2009. http://0-search .ebscohost.com.helin.uri.edu.

This article provides statistics and graphs depicting who the victims of sex trafficking are, where they come from and where they will be trafficked to, how large of an issue trafficking is, the impacts on victims, and other important facts to know about sex trafficking. This article is the most relevant to my research topic of all the sources I have found. It directly answers my question and provides reliable statistical information. This article is not attributed to one specific author but to the journal *New Internationalist.* This journal appears to be a special-interest journal; however, I still believe it is a reliable source as it cites other sources and has been in publication for over thirty years.

Polaris Project. *Polaris Project: For a World without Slavery.* 6 April 2009. Polaris Project. 13 April 2009. www.polarisproject.org/component/option,com _frontpage/Itemid,1/.

Polaris Project: For a World without Slavery is the official website for Polaris Project, one of the largest anti-trafficking organizations in Japan and the United States. The website details the actions that are being taken by Polaris Project in the hopes of eradicating human trafficking by providing the website's viewers with information regarding national and local outreach programs, factual information regarding human trafficking, and opportunities to donate or become involved with the organization. The one page that I found to be particularly relevant to my research was a page titled "Action Center: Survivor Testimonies." This area of the website is extremely useful to me as my research is focused on the victims of sex trafficking and the page provides firsthand accounts of sexual exploitation from actual trafficked victims. I believe the website is credible as it is run by an extremely reputable organization; is frequently updated, well maintained, professional; and does not seek to profit personally but seeks only to help victims.

Shelley, Louise. "Trafficking in Women: The Business Model Approach." *Brown Journal of World Affairs* 10.1 (2003): 119–131. Women's Studies International. University of Rhode Island. University Library, Kingston, RI. 23 March 2009. http://0-search .ebscohost.com.helin.uri.edu.

This article explores sex trafficking from a business perspective, including how crime groups profit and function in the sex trade. It also explores the recent increase of trafficked women. This article is relevant to my research topic because it helps me understand one of the reasons why victims are trafficked. Looking at trafficking from a business perspective, one can easily see how crime groups can profit from the trade. This article is found in a nonprofit, scholarly journal distributed by Brown University, and the information seems to be well researched and up-to-date. The author is a professor in the Department of Justice, Law, and Society as well as the founder-director of the Transnational Crime and Corruption Center.

Sorajjakool, Siroj. *Child Prostitution in Thailand: Listening to Rahab.* New York: Haworth Press, 2003.

This book was inspired by author Siroj Sorajjakool's attempt to understand the sex industry that surrounded him where he grew up in Bangkok. To better understand the sex trade, Sorajjakool traveled to Thailand and conducted a series of research that has come together to form this book. The book explores who the victims of the sex trade are, how the market works, and even who the perpetrators are. The book provides statistics, facts, and figures, as well as personal stories of victims in Thailand. Sorajjakool is an associate professor of religion at Loma Linda University and was associate director of the Adventist Development and Relief Agency in Thailand. He earned his PhD in theology and personality and his MA in theological studies. In the preface of his book, Sorajjakool gives the reader some understanding of the extensive research he conducted to write the book, and he includes bibliographic information in the back of the book. He seems to be a credible source as he is an eyewitness to the sex trade industry in Thailand. This book is a useful source as the information is current and accurate and provides a different perspective on the sex trade industry, focusing particularly on children. The book encompasses a great deal of information and provides some answers to my research question.

SwirlyGig Media. *Captive Daughters: Dedicated to Ending Sex Trafficking.* 2005. Captive Daughters. 13 April 2009. www.captivedaughters.org/index.htm.

This website is the official website for Captive Daughters, a nonprofit organization dedicated to ending the trafficking of women and children for sexual exploitation by educating the public, raising awareness, and strengthening the anti-trafficking movement. It provides website visitors with general facts and information regarding sex trafficking, legislation regarding human rights, additional resources, and opportunities to donate and volunteer. The page that is most relevant to my research topic is titled "Cause: Demand," and it answers the second part of my research question by citing the cause of sex trafficking. I believe this website is a valuable source as it is run by a credible nonprofit organization, is informative and useful to my research, and cites a great deal of credible, outside sources. It also links to other resources such as articles, books, and films that would be useful for further research.

Yen, Iris. "Of Vice and Men: A New Approach to Eradicating Sex Trafficking by Reducing Male Demand through Educational Programs and Abolitionist Legislation." *Journal of Criminal Law and Criminology* 98.2 (2008): 653–686. Women's Studies International. University of Rhode Island. University Library, Kingston, RI. 23 March 2009. http://0-search .ebscohost.com.helin.uri.edu.

This article explores the male perspective of sex trafficking, including why there is a male demand for trafficked women and how this demand can be deterred through educational programming. This article is relevant to my research as it shows the demand side of the sex industry and why the sex industry is continuing to grow. This partially answers my research question on why victims become victims of sex trafficking. The journal that printed this article, the *Journal of Criminal Law and Criminology,* is a scholarly journal produced by the Northwestern University School of Law. Iris Yen is a student at Northwestern University School of Law and has a BA in international studies and a BS in economics.

Annotated Bibliography of Nonrelevant Sources

Laczko, Frank, and Elzbieta Gozdziak, eds. *Data and Research on Human Trafficking: A Global Survey*. Geneva: International Organization for Migration, 2005.

This book offers current research and data on human trafficking around the globe, and it features nine articles that focus on trafficking in specific regions. The book also contains articles that explore issues relating to research methods, particularly how these methods can be improved and what their current strengths and weaknesses are. If I were to use

this source for a research paper, it would be extremely useful in providing the convincing factual evidence and statistics that an audience looks for from a reliable research paper. The data would provide documented support and proof for my claims, and as the book was just published in 2005, the data is still fairly current. The book also provides an extensive bibliography that is organized by region, and although there is no one author (there are two editors), the articles were compiled by a reliable authority: the International Organization for Migration. Overall, this source seems to meet all the evaluative criteria for a relevant source.

I chose not to include this source because it focuses primarily on improving methods for researching sex trafficking, and it is not particularly helpful in answering my research question.

Tiefenbrun, Susan W. "Updating the Domestic and International Impact of the U.S. Victims of Trafficking Protection Act of 2000: Does Law Deter Crime?" *Case Western Reserve Journal of International Law* 38.2 (Aug. 2006): 249–280. Academic Search Premier. EBSCO. University of Rhode Island. University Library, Kingston, RI. 25 Feb. 2009. http://0-search.ebscohost .com.helin.uri.edu/login.aspx?direct=true&db=aph& AN=25753594&site=ehost-live.

This article also explores the issue of sex trafficking from a criminal law perspective and questions whether sex trafficking laws actually discourage sex trafficking crimes from being committed. This article is useful to my research because it provides background information, including who the victims of sex trafficking are, and facts and statistics regarding sex trafficking. As my topic questions how victims fall into the sex trade industry, the article's discussion of whether sex trafficking laws effectively prevent trafficking will shed light on this issue. The author, Susan W. Tiefenbrun, is a professor of law as well as the director of the Center for Global Legal Studies at the Thomas Jefferson School of Law. This case appears in a law journal, and like my other sources, it is a scholarly journal.

I chose not to use this article for my research because it primarily focuses on sex trafficking from a legal standpoint, and although it is a good article, the legality of sex trafficking is not the primary focus of my research question.

Weitzer, Ronald, ed. *Sex for Sale: Prostitution, Pornography, and the Sex Industry*. New York: Routledge, 2000.

This book explores prostitution, pornography, and the sex industry in three parts. The first part,

"Perspectives of Sex Workers and Customers," explores the motivation behind sex work as well as the motivation of the clients. The second part of the book, "Victimization, Risk Behavior, and Support Services," explores the physical and health risks inherent with prostitution and sex work as well as the outlets that workers can turn to for help. The final section of the book, "Politics, Policing, and the Sex Industry," looks at the legal aspects of sex work. The editor, Ronald Weitzer, is an associate professor of sociology at George Washington University and received his PhD from the University of California at Berkeley. He is also the author of two other books. The back of the book provides a list of contributors and their credentials as well as bibliographic information and a list of other recommended readings that make me believe that the book is accurate and well researched. This source is a relevant source as it provides different perspectives of sex work (the workers and their clients) as well as legal information on prostitution in the United States. The book is also less than ten years old, so general information (perhaps not statistics) is still current and relevant.

This is one of the first sources I found, and it seemed useful to my research at the time, but I discovered later in the research process that sex trafficking and prostitution are not the same thing, and I have therefore decided not to include this source.

Research Journal

Entry: Encyclopedia

Before I searched for this encyclopedia in the URI library, I searched the online HELIN catalog over the weekend, using a number of different search terms (such as *human/sex trafficking, prostitution, exploitation, servitude,* etc.) as well as the word *encyclopedia*. I used the term *AND* to link the terms. I was somewhat frustrated by the search when it yielded only two results, even though I had tried every combination of terms I could think of and even resorted to using a thesaurus to find similar words. I was hoping to have more options in case I had difficulty finding one or both of the sources or they had already been checked out by another student. After extensive searching on the HELIN catalog, I decided I wasn't going to be able to find another subject-specific encyclopedia, and I wrote the call numbers down for both encyclopedias and took the list to the library. I searched for the encyclopedia in the reference section in the library and was unable to find my first source. I searched for the encyclopedia I have chosen to use as my source after I had no luck with the first source. After I found the right section, the encyclopedia was fairly

easy to find. I then searched the index and found the article that seemed most relevant to my topic (there were also a number of other articles that would also be useful). I chose the article "Human Trafficking" as the more useful article for my research (in comparison to the article "Sex and Sexuality") because it seemed to answer or address a number of the questions that I had generated using the concept map. The article "Sex and Sexuality" only briefly and barely touched on anything close to my research topic. I had difficulty finding anything relevant to my topic in the general encyclopedias and found that the subject-specific encyclopedia was much more useful. The article "Human Trafficking" is entirely relevant to my topic and provided me with information that I was not already familiar with.

Entry: Books

The first research step I took for the "Annotated Bibliography of Books" assignment was to use the HELIN catalog keyword search to find books relevant to my topic. Using the keywords I had generated with the "Concept Mapping" assignment, I found a number of options for books. I looked at the bibliographic record for each of these books and located the LC Subject for each of the books I found. Using these subjects, I searched the HELIN catalog again and generated even more sources. I printed out about ten of these sources and took them to the library with me. I located the area on the third floor, where most of the call numbers for my books were located. While searching for my books, I met another student who was using the same research topic for another section of Library 120. We decided to look for our books together, as we were looking for many of the same books. Unfortunately, neither of us was able to find any of the books on our list, so we went to the reference desk and asked a librarian to steer us in the right direction. She helped us find the books we were looking for in a row that we had not seen. We were both frustrated trying to find the books we needed as there were two rows that started with the proper call number (HQ) and another row with the same call number (HQ) that was not in succession with the rows we had been searching in. However, after being steered in the right direction, I was able to find all the books I had been searching for as well as a number of other books relevant to my topic. Once I had asked for help from a librarian, and had the help of another student, my search process was fairly straightforward.

Entry: Academic Search Premier

The first step I took in my research process was to use the keywords I had generated from my concept map to search Academic Search Premier. For the first time I searched, I chose not to use any of the limitation functions that the database offers. I wanted to first see how many results the database would find. I searched using the term *sex trafficking,* which returned a number of results. However, I found that many of the results did not offer the full text, and I could not locate many of the articles using HELIN. Additionally, many of the results that did offer full text were not entirely relevant to my research topic. I decided to search again using the term *human trafficking* as the issue of sex trafficking is often discussed with human trafficking. This search yielded more results, and many of the results seemed more relevant to my topic than those I had found searching with the term *sex trafficking.* I decided to limit my search by searching only for scholarly journals. This narrowed my search greatly, but there were still a number of scholarly articles on the issue of human trafficking that did not offer full text that I could locate. As the database had returned a number of articles, I decided to limit my search further by searching for articles that were greater than two pages in length. Using these searching techniques, I found four sources that were relevant to my research question. I used the abstracts provided and read the first few pages of each article to determine their relevance. I was primarily searching for articles that discussed the victims of sex trafficking. The articles I found elaborate on who the victims are, how the legal system can help them, and how flaws in the legal system can also result in increased or uncontrolled trade of men, women, and children into the sex industry. Once I had found four relevant and peer-reviewed articles, I used the information I had gathered in determining the article's relevance to create my annotations. I used the template provided by Academic Search Premier as well as the book I have from one of my writing classes, *MLA Handbook for Writers of Research Papers,* to cite the sources. I searched the Internet for some of the websites of the journals the articles were published in to make sure they were actually credible and scholarly. I had some difficulty finding one of the authors, Jennifer Nam, but after finding the website of the journal her article was published in, I determined that the author was likely a student at Columbia Law School. Other than this, the process seemed to go well.

Entry: Subject-Specific Databases

The first step I took in my research process was to scan the different categories of reference databases and find categories that looked like they would pertain to my research question. I first looked under Government, Politics, & Law. I looked at the description for each subject-specific database and chose a few that seemed relevant. I then typed my keywords into each of these databases. None of the databases that seemed relevant yielded any

results. I found this surprising as sex trafficking is a criminal act and is outlawed. I went back to the category page for reference databases and decided to search under Social Sciences. I followed much the same process as I did with the previous databases. I chose databases that seemed relevant and searched with my keywords. I wasn't surprised to find a number of options using the Women's Studies International database, as sex trafficking is an issue that affects primarily women. I searched through twelve pages of results and found three articles that appeared to meet my criteria. The articles answer my research question or a part of it, were scholarly and/or credible, and were at least three pages in length. I then went back to the Social Sciences section and found another database whose description looked relevant. The Social Services Abstracts database yielded fewer results than the previous database, but I was still able to find an article that met my criteria as the others had. When citing these articles, I used the handout provided in class for citing articles found through online reference databases. For the annotation of each article, I searched for the websites of each journal online to ensure that the journals were credible and also to determine what type of publication each was. I did the same for two of the authors whose credentials weren't listed in the print record or first page of the article. I read the first few pages of each article as well as the abstract provided in the full record to create my annotation. I had some difficulty comparing the two databases. Although they were somewhat different, they are both concerned with social sciences and they yielded many of the same results. Both databases were similar except perhaps the target audience was different; for instance, the Women's Studies International database was geared more toward women and feminists.

Entry: Websites

For this assignment, I chose to use two different search engines that we had learned about in class but that I'm not particularly familiar with. I chose to use Dogpile and Exalead.com/search because they seemed to be valuable search engines. I first searched with Exalead by typing my keywords *sex trafficking* into the search box. My search generated a number of results, but many of these were only individual pages dedicated to sex trafficking rather than entire websites. I chose to use the advanced search feature to narrow my results. As I familiarized myself with the advanced search feature, I noticed a tool that allowed me to choose where my information would come from. One of these options was "in title of page" and had the word *website* in parentheses next to it. I clicked this feature, and it added the following text to the search bar: *intitle:(sex trafficking).* Using this phrasing, my search became more focused, returning primarily entire websites dedicated to the topic of sex trafficking. I looked at a number of these websites; however, many were run by religious organizations and did not seem to be unbiased or credible sources. Yet I did find one website, Captive Daughters.org, which looked promising. I browsed the website, particularly the About Us section, and determined that it met my evaluation criteria. Unlike many of the other websites, it was run by a nonprofit organization, was well researched and organized, and did not appear to have any bias. I also found in my browsing that the website helped to answer my research question. For these reasons I chose to use this website as one of my sources.

I chose to use Dogpile for the remainder of my search after sifting through a number of pages on Exalead and having difficulty locating any more valuable sources using that search engine. I began my search on Dogpile using the same keywords in the search bar, *sex trafficking*. I scanned the first two pages of results, looking in particular at the website address listed under each entry. Many of these addresses indicated that the result was only a single page. To return better results I decided to use the feature located on the right-hand side of the search engine, "Are you looking for?" Similar to subject terms, this feature listed a number of phrases related to the term *sex trafficking*, such as "Causes in Human Trafficking," "Facts about Human Trafficking," etc. I browsed these phrases and searched using a number of them, again paying close attention to the site address. Doing this I was able to locate three more relevant sources. I used the same search criteria to determine the value of each website as I had for the Captive Daughters.org website. I also browsed the websites to find information that was directly relevant to my research question. Each of the websites I chose answers all or part of my research question. I found that Dogpile returned more valuable results than Exalead, perhaps because it is a metasearch engine.

Research Summary

Part 1: Information Need

Over the course of the semester I found quite a few sources that addressed my research question. These sources came from a number of different literary forms, and although some were more useful than others, I believe that if I had to write a research paper utilizing these sources it would be well supported and thorough. I certainly found enough

information to answer my research question. I would like to have found a bit more to address the "how do they become victims" part of my question; however, I have enough information that it can be answered thoughtfully. Overall, I believe I found relevant and useful sources.

Part 2: Information Literacy

I did not come into this class thinking that it would require as much hard work as it did, and as a junior, I thought I was sufficiently able to locate relevant sources from a number of different locations and databases. I quickly discovered that there was much I needed to learn about the research process. Although the research process required a lot of effort, I think that, overall, the process went smoothly and I learned a great deal along the way. I now am comfortable not only finding sources but determining their relevance as well. The hardest task in this process was retrieving sources from online databases, and it is in this area that I feel I have progressed the most. I am now comfortable not only using a number of different databases but also using the tools I have learned over the course of the semester, such as Boolean searching and truncation when searching these databases. I also found it difficult to locate books within the library using call numbers. Now I feel that if I need to locate a book, I will be able to do so successfully. I felt the easiest part of the research process was preparing the annotations. After the sources were found, the annotations were simple to create. The best sources I found were the websites and books. The database articles were useful because they tended to address one specific issue; however, the books and websites addressed quite a few issues and provided more information in total. In general, I feel that I have learned more about the research process than I had ever expected, and this class has certainly changed the way I will conduct research in the future. I now realize that before this class, I was not finding credible and relevant sources, and I was also limiting the sources I could find by only using one search method. Now, however, I realize that I have a number of search tools at my disposal. If I could give one piece of advice to a non–Library 120 student, it would be to become familiar with the library's databases and search tips. It is easy nowadays when the Internet is so useful to just search using search engines such as Google. Although I have learned that these search engines can be helpful, I have also discovered that there is so much information that can be found using other sources.

Student Time Line for Completing the Paper Trail Project

This time line is based on implementing the Paper Trail Project during a fifteen-week information literacy course.

Week 1: General Introduction to the Paper Trail Project

In class: Students discuss Paper Trail Project goal and objectives and receive handout describing the requirements for the project.

Out of class: Students brainstorm and jot down three ideas that can be developed into topics for their Paper Trail Projects.

Week 2: Choosing a Topic

In class: Students identify and locate encyclopedias during class time. Students use instructor-provided guide to practice writing encyclopedia citations and annotations. Students receive instruction on how to write research journal entries.

Out of class: Students find an encyclopedia article on their topic, create a citation and annotation for the article, and write a research journal entry about the process.

Week 3: Developing the Research Question

In class: Students create a concept map for their topic. Students use worksheets to develop possible Paper Trail research questions.

Out of class: Students develop finalized Paper Trail Project research questions and write a research journal entry on the process.

Week 4: Finding and Using Books

In class: Students search the catalog and retrieve books relevant to their topics.

Week 5: Developing an Annotated Bibliography of Books

In class: Using instructor-provided guide and verbal instructions, students learn to prepare a formal "Annotated Bibliography of Books."

Out of class: Students complete a five-item "Annotated Bibliography of Books," writing research journal entries for each item.

Week 6: Finding and Using Print Periodical Literature

In class: Students practice using print indexes to identify citations. Students practice locating articles using the library catalog.

Out of class: Students identify, read, and evaluate several periodical articles from print indexes for their Paper Trail Projects.

Week 7: Finding and Using Electronic Periodical Literature

In class: Students practice using online periodical databases to identify relevant periodical citations for their Paper Trail Projects. Students practice using evaluative criteria to judge the appropriateness of articles for their projects.

Out of class: Students use electronic periodical databases to identify and locate five relevant articles on their Paper Trail topic.

Week 8: Developing an Annotated Bibliography of Articles

In class: Using the guide provided, students practice writing periodical citations and annotations.

Out of class: Students develop and write a five-item "Annotated Bibliography of Periodical Articles" on their topic and include research journal entries for each.

Week 9: Using Experts and Statistics in Research

In class: Students practice using library tools to identify experts and statistics on their topics.

Out of class: Students identify and contact three experts, asking for information for their research; and/or students identify and cite three supportive statistics for their Paper Trail Project. Students write research journal entries for "Experts and Statistics."

Week 10: Finding Websites for Research

In class: Students explore and practice using effective web-searching techniques to find quality websites related to their topics.

Out of class: Students select several websites and describe their content and usefulness in journal entries. Students continue to identify, obtain, and evaluate relevant books, articles, expert information, statistics, and websites and comment on what they have found in their journal entries.

Week 11: Evaluating Websites for Research

In class: Students evaluate their selected websites based on criteria discussed in class. Students practice writing citations and annotations for websites.

Out of class: Students develop and write a five-item "Annotated Bibliography of Websites," including research journal entries for each website used.

Week 12: Putting It All Together

In class: Students meet with the instructor to review Paper Trail Project progress.

Out of class: Students revise, update, and complete Paper Trail Project parts.

Weeks 13 and 14: Finalizing the Project

In class: The instructor wraps up the semester by reviewing topics and applying assessments.

Out of class: Students complete and finalize projects outside of class. Students contact the instructor via e-mail or phone for guidance.

Week 15: Paper Trail Project Completed

In class: All projects turned in today!

Chapter Eleven
Assessment

Assessment is what shows us how well our message or lesson was received and remembered by our students. It demonstrates student success and learning. The best methods of assessment require students to use, apply, and/or translate what they have learned to complete a task or assignment. Assessments can be complex or simple, long-term or short-term. By asking students to explain what they have learned, their deep learning (deep learning is the learning that has been "hardwired" in the brain over the course of the semester; it has been thoroughly learned and incorporated into the core of what the student knows without really thinking about it), long-term retention, and ability to transfer concepts to new applications can be assessed.

Assessment is part of the "feedback cycle of learning." In addition to telling students how well they have learned, the results of assessments will show instructors where *they* have been successful in transferring knowledge to students and where there is a need for improvement. This second piece of the process of assessment should result in adjustments to the lesson if needed. If the assessment cycle is completed, lessons should go through adjustments and changes until they are balanced with student outcomes that meet a preset benchmark (80 percent of the class scores a C or better on the assessment, for example).

In addition to its other uses, assessment allows students to practice and use what they know. Long-term retention of information requires repeated application of that information. Using a variety of assessment types accommodates different learning styles and allows students to use different methods and skills in completing the assessment. As part of the learning cycle, students can solidify their long-term retention by applying what they have learned while completing an assessment.

HOW DOES ONE CREATE AN ASSESSMENT?

It is useful to create an assessment at the same time you are planning a lesson, as the two are almost inseparable. In planning for any lesson, its important set a goal (or outcome) by asking the question "What do I want the students to learn or take away from this lesson?" This goal should be the instructor's guide for both presenting the lesson and assessing it. Once the goal has been established, it is then necessary to ask, "How can I determine whether or how well the students received and remembered the lesson?"

There are many types of assessment. Not every type of assessment is applicable to every learning situation. However, each is effective if used properly. In some situations it is useful to use more than one type of assessment, especially to address different learning styles.

Tests and Quizzes. Most instructors are familiar with testing students by asking them to answer questions on paper (or online). Tests can include matching, multiple choice, short answer, and essay or a combination of these techniques. These kinds of questions generally test memory, but they may not get to the heart of whether or not the student has internalized the information for use in deep learning.

Some other methods of assessment require students to use, apply, and/or translate what they have learned to complete a task or assignment. These assessments can be simple or complex. They can be long term or short term. By asking students to explain what they have learned, their deep learning, long-term retention, and ability to transfer concepts to new applications can be assessed, rather than simply their ability to memorize. Some other methods of assessment follow:

Minute Writing. Ask students to reflect in a time-limited situation on a reading or concept. Ask one question that requires the students to explain or apply what they have learned. This writing should be no longer than one or two minutes.

Muddiest Point. At the end of a lesson, ask students to write down the part of the lesson that is least clear to them or about which they still have questions.

Peer Teaching. Place students in pairs or small groups and have one student teach the other(s) what he or she learned in the lesson.

Practical Application. Have students complete an assignment that requires the use of the information presented in the lesson by using it in a new way. For example, if the lesson has been about the evaluation of websites, ask students to select a website on a specific topic and defend its use as an appropriate academic source for a term paper or an appropriate source for a personal application. If the lesson has been about how to use the advanced search options in a database, have them examine the advanced search options in a new database and compare the two.

Class Presentation. Although most students do not enjoy being in the spotlight giving a class presentation, the process of finding the information, putting it into a logical and understandable format, and presenting it to an audience is something most students will be called upon to do in their working lives. It is beneficial for students to have practice in this type of assessment in class, where the stakes are not as high as they might be in the workplace. Class presentations can be done by individuals or small groups. They can be presented in a variety of ways. Students might use technology to enhance the presentation. Have students do some research and present their findings to the class. Require a handout and/or a bibliography of their research.

Annotation. Have students summarize in writing the reading or lesson they have just completed, pointing out the most important points.

Portfolio with Written Reflection. Have students save their work in a portfolio (paper or electronic) and periodically reflect on what they have learned and how their learning has progressed over a period of time.

Comprehensive Exam. The comprehensive exam should assess the total learning achieved by students by including a variety of questions requiring the application of what they have learned in class. It should give students the opportunity to explain, demonstrate, produce, and apply information in a variety of ways. This is also a possible means of comparing one group of students to another (see the "Comprehensive Exam" description below).

LONG-TERM LEARNING AND RETENTION

Long-term learning and retention are most successful when students

- get feedback,
- have the ability to revise and redo, and
- reapply skills/knowledge in a new way.

To maximize student success, process assessments so that students get feedback on what they have done well, what needs work, and how they can do better. Having students submit assignments they never see again, or returning assignments with no accompanying feedback, may fulfill the instructors need to measure student learning. It does not, however, allow the student to learn from their mistakes or to reinforce their correct answers.

This means that scheduling is an important part of assessment. With a long-term project like a term paper, it is often difficult for students to gauge how well or how poorly they have done. Because a term paper is usually due at the end of the term, there is little time for feedback and no time for revision.

However, a large project like a term paper could be broken down into smaller tasks that can be assessed before the whole project is due, allowing students time to receive feedback and to revise and apply as appropriate. Examples of some other large projects are listed below.

Paper Trail Project

Portfolio

Capstone Project (a final summative project drawing together what the student has learned and showing mastery of the subject)

Senior Thesis

RUBRICS

Students should know what elements of the assignment they will be graded on and how much weight each element carries. This requires the construction of a rubric for each assignment. Rubrics can be simple or complex. They should be based on the desired learning outcomes for the assignment they relate to, which must, of course, be determined in advance.

In essence, the stated goal for the exercise or assignment will break down into measurable components for the completion of the assignment. Each component is assigned a value, and students are rated (and earn points) based on how well they have met the requirements for each component. Scores for each component are totaled for a grade for the assignment or exercise.

We have provided the rubric we use for the Paper Trail Project in a three-credit course in information literacy as an example (see chapter 10, figure 10.1, "Grading Rubric for the Paper Trail Project").

Rubrics should be given to students with the assignment, to show them how their assessment will be graded. The rubric serves as a standardized means of assigning points and allows the instructor to determine

the extent to which the learning outcomes/goals have been met.

TIPS FOR USING ASSESSMENTS

Process and return assessments with comments, so that students get feedback on what they have done well, what needs work, and how they can do better.

Use the results of each assessment to evaluate how well the assignment/exercise achieved its goals. If students did not perform as expected, it's a clear indicator that the assignment/exercise needs adjustment or revision.

COMPREHENSIVE EXAM

In teaching information literacy, we wanted to be able to provide information to ourselves and to the administration that our course was valuable to students and worth the time, personnel, and equipment required. To accomplish this, we wanted all students who took Library 120 to take the same comprehensive exam. This exam would test their proficiency in information literacy, using a variety of testing methods and requiring students to apply what they learned to new situations.

Administration of a common exam was not difficult. We used the classroom management software (CMS) the university supported. We scheduled common exam times each semester. We had paper backup exams, in case of catastrophic computer failure on campus. We had computer technicians on hand in case of minor computer problems. Students came in person to take the exam on library computers.

We did not feel we had the expertise or the time to create our own testing instrument. We also hoped to find an instrument that others were using. This would allow us to assess our students and compare the results of their testing to those of other institutions. Finding a comprehensive exam that met our needs was a little more difficult. Although there were several field-tested assessments of information literacy available, only one met our criteria. The Bay Area Community College Information Competency Assessment Project allowed us to use and modify their exam.

The instruction group met weekly for several months, using grant money to fund several retreats to work exclusively on the comprehensive exam.

We identified questions that needed adjustment. We debated the wording, the type of question, the examples chosen, and so on. Once we had our testing instrument drafted, we asked a small group of graduate students to field test it for us. Their test results and their comments allowed us to revise and fine-tune the exam. When it had been edited, we asked another small group of graduate students to take the test and to give us feedback on what problems they had in taking the exam.

Meanwhile, we worked out the logistics of where and when the exam would be given and made contingency plans for anything that might go wrong. The students first took the comprehensive exam at the end of the fall semester 2006. The exam counted as 10 percent of their final grade. For our own purposes, we set a benchmark of 70 percent as the lowest passing grade. We were able to determine from this benchmark how many students scored above or below this benchmark.

The answers for each question were analyzed to show how many students got each question right or wrong. Because the exam questions were mapped to the ACRL "Information Literacy Competency Standards for Higher Education, Standards, Performance Indicators, and Outcomes," we also used summary information to determine whether there were standards that were not being met by our course. Finally, we used the summarized student results to determine if there were questions that were problematic because they were poorly worded or hard to understand for some other reason.

After the first administration of the exam, the instructors group met again to go over the results, determine which questions needed adjustment, and rewrite the problem questions. The revised exam was given again in the spring semester. This cycle continued until summer 2009. At this time, we felt we had collected enough data to show that the course was valuable to the student, that most students were at least meeting the benchmark grade set, and to alert us to problem areas in our teaching. We continue to use the data to assess how our students perform and where improvements can be made in our course.

We feel that the comprehensive exam is a valuable tool when used in concert with the Paper Trail Project. Together, these two assessments allow us to determine student learning outcomes, teaching outcomes, and outcomes for the information literacy program.

Information Literacy Competency Standards for Higher Education

Association of College and Research Libraries, "Information Literacy Competency Standards for Higher Education, Standards, Performance Indicators, and Outcomes." Approved by ACRL Board, January 18, 2000.

STANDARD ONE

The information-literate student determines the nature and extent of the information needed.

Performance Indicators

1. The information-literate student defines and articulates the need for information.

Outcomes Include

    a. Confers with instructors and participates in class discussions, peer work-groups, and electronic discussions to identify a research topic or other information need

    b. Develops a thesis statement and formulates questions based on the information need

    c. Explores general information sources to increase familiarity with the topic

    d. Defines or modifies the information need to achieve a manageable focus

    e. Identifies key concepts and terms that describe the information need

    f. Recognizes that existing information can be combined with original thought, experimentation, and/or analysis to produce new information

2. The information-literate student identifies a variety of types and formats of potential sources for information.

Outcomes Include

    a. Knows how information is formally and informally produced, organized, and disseminated

b. Recognizes that knowledge can be organized into disciplines that influence the way information is accessed

c. Identifies the value and differences of potential resources in a variety of formats (e.g., multimedia, database, website, data set, audio/visual, book)

d. Identifies the purpose and audience of potential resources (e.g., popular vs. scholarly, current vs. historical)

e. Differentiates between primary and secondary sources, recognizing how their use and importance vary with each discipline

f. Realizes that information may need to be constructed with raw data from primary sources

3. The information-literate student considers the costs and benefits of acquiring the needed information.

Outcomes Include

a. Determines the availability of needed information and makes decisions on broadening the information-seeking process beyond local resources (e.g., interlibrary loan; using resources at other locations; obtaining images, videos, text, or sound)

b. Considers the feasibility of acquiring a new language or skill (e.g., foreign or discipline-based) in order to gather needed information and to understand its context

c. Defines a realistic overall plan and time line to acquire the needed information

4. The information-literate student reevaluates the nature and extent of the information need.

Outcomes Include

a. Reviews the initial information need to clarify, revise, or refine the question

b. Describes criteria used to make information decisions and choices

STANDARD TWO

The information-literate student accesses needed information effectively and efficiently.

Performance Indicators

1. The information-literate student selects the most appropriate investigative methods or information retrieval systems for accessing the needed information.

Outcomes Include

a. Identifies appropriate investigative methods (e.g., laboratory experiment, simulation, fieldwork)

b. Investigates benefits and applicability of various investigative methods

c. Investigates the scope, content, and organization of information retrieval systems

d. Selects efficient and effective approaches for accessing the information needed from the investigative method or information retrieval system

2. The information-literate student constructs and implements effectively designed search strategies.

Outcomes Include

a. Develops a research plan appropriate to the investigative method

b. Identifies keywords, synonyms, and related terms for the information needed

c. Selects controlled vocabulary specific to the discipline or information retrieval source

d. Constructs a search strategy using appropriate commands for the information retrieval system selected (e.g., Boolean operators, truncation, and proximity for search engines; internal organizers such as indexes for books)

e. Implements the search strategy in various information retrieval systems using different user interfaces and search engines, with different command languages, protocols, and search parameters

f. Implements the search using investigative protocols appropriate to the discipline

3. *The information-literate student retrieves information online or in person using a variety of methods.*

Outcomes Include

a. Uses various search systems to retrieve information in a variety of formats

b. Uses various classification schemes and other systems (e.g., call number systems or indexes) to locate information resources within the library or to identify specific sites for physical exploration

c. Uses specialized online or in-person services available at the institution to retrieve information needed (e.g., interlibrary loan/document delivery, professional associations, institutional research offices, community resources, experts and practitioners)

d. Uses surveys, letters, interviews, and other forms of inquiry to retrieve primary information

4. *The information-literate student refines the search strategy if necessary.*

Outcomes Include

a. Assesses the quantity, quality, and relevance of the search results to determine whether alternative information retrieval systems or investigative methods should be utilized

b. Identifies gaps in the information retrieved and determines if the search strategy should be revised

c. Repeats the search using the revised strategy as necessary

5. *The information-literate student extracts, records, and manages the information and its sources.*

Outcomes Include

a. Selects among various technologies the most appropriate one for the task of extracting the needed information (e.g., copy/paste software functions, photocopier, scanner, audio/visual equipment, or exploratory instruments)

b. Creates a system for organizing the information

c. Differentiates between the types of sources cited and understands the elements and correct syntax of a citation for a wide range of resources

d. Records all pertinent citation information for future reference

e. Uses various technologies to manage the information selected and organized

STANDARD THREE

The information-literate student evaluates information and its sources critically and incorporates selected information into his or her knowledge base and value system.

Performance Indicators

1. *The information-literate student summarizes the main ideas to be extracted from the information gathered.*

Outcomes Include

a. Reads the text and selects main ideas

b. Restates textual concepts in his/her own words and selects data accurately

c. Identifies verbatim material that can be then appropriately quoted

2. *The information-literate student articulates and applies initial criteria for evaluating both the information and its sources.*

Outcomes Include

a. Examines and compares information from various sources in order to evaluate reliability, validity, accuracy, authority, timeliness, and point of view or bias

b. Analyzes the structure and logic of supporting arguments or methods

c. Recognizes prejudice, deception, or manipulation

d. Recognizes the cultural, physical, or other context within which the information was created and understands the impact of context on interpreting the information

3. *The information-literate student synthesizes main ideas to construct new concepts.*

Outcomes Include

    a. Recognizes interrelationships among concepts and combines them into potentially useful primary statements with supporting evidence

    b. Extends initial synthesis, when possible, at a higher level of abstraction to construct new hypotheses that may require additional information

    c. Utilizes computer and other technologies (e.g., spreadsheets, databases, multimedia, and audio or visual equipment) for studying the interaction of ideas and other phenomena

4. *The information-literate student compares new knowledge with prior knowledge to determine the value added, contradictions, or other unique characteristics of the information.*

Outcomes Include

    a. Determines whether information satisfies the research or other information need

    b. Uses consciously selected criteria to determine whether the information contradicts or verifies information used from other sources

    c. Draws conclusions based upon information gathered

    d. Tests theories with discipline-appropriate techniques (e.g., simulators, experiments)

    e. Determines probable accuracy by questioning the source of the data, the limitations of the information gathering tools or strategies, and the reasonableness of the conclusions

    f. Integrates new information with previous information or knowledge

    g. Selects information that provides evidence for the topic

5. *The information-literate student determines whether the new knowledge has an impact on the individual's value system and takes steps to reconcile differences.*

Outcomes Include

    a. Investigates differing viewpoints encountered in the literature

    b. Determines whether to incorporate or reject viewpoints encountered

6. *The information-literate student validates understanding and interpretation of the information through discourse with other individuals, subject-area experts, and/or practitioners.*

Outcomes Include

    a. Participates in classroom and other discussions

    b. Participates in class-sponsored electronic communication forums designed to encourage discourse on the topic (e.g., e-mail, bulletin boards, chat rooms)

    c. Seeks expert opinion through a variety of mechanisms (e.g., interviews, e-mail, listservs)

7. *The information-literate student determines whether the initial query should be revised.*

Outcomes Include

    a. Determines if original information need has been satisfied or if additional information is needed

    b. Reviews search strategy and incorporates additional concepts as necessary

    c. Reviews information retrieval sources used and expands to include others as needed

STANDARD FOUR

The information-literate student, individually or as a member of a group, uses information effectively to accomplish a specific purpose.

Performance Indicators

1. The information-literate student applies new and prior information to the planning and creation of a particular product or performance.

Outcomes Include

    a. Organizes the content in a manner that supports the purposes and format of the product or performance (e.g., outlines, drafts, storyboards)

    b. Articulates knowledge and skills transferred from prior experiences to planning and creating the product or performance

    c. Integrates the new and prior information, including quotations and paraphrasings, in a manner that supports the purposes of the product or performance

    d. Manipulates digital text, images, and data as needed, transferring them from their original locations and formats to a new context

2. The information-literate student revises the development process for the product or performance.

Outcomes Include

    a. Maintains a journal or log of activities related to the information-seeking, evaluating, and communicating process

    b. Reflects on past successes, failures, and alternative strategies

3. The information-literate student communicates the product or performance effectively to others.

Outcomes Include

    a. Chooses a communication medium and format that best supports the purposes of the product or performance and the intended audience

    b. Uses a range of information technology applications in creating the product or performance

    c. Incorporates principles of design and communication

    d. Communicates clearly and with a style that supports the purposes of the intended audience

STANDARD FIVE

The information-literate student understands many of the economic, legal, and social issues surrounding the use of information and accesses and uses information ethically and legally.

Performance Indicators

1. The information-literate student understands many of the ethical, legal and socio-economic issues surrounding information and information technology.

Outcomes Include

    a. Identifies and discusses issues related to privacy and security in both the print and electronic environments

    b. Identifies and discusses issues related to free vs. fee-based access to information

    c. Identifies and discusses issues related to censorship and freedom of speech

    d. Demonstrates an understanding of intellectual property, copyright, and fair use of copyrighted material

2. The information-literate student follows laws, regulations, institutional policies, and etiquette related to the access and use of information resources.

Outcomes Include

    a. Participates in electronic discussions following accepted practices (e.g., "netiquette")

    b. Uses approved passwords and other forms of ID for access to information resources

    c. Complies with institutional policies on access to information resources

    d. Preserves the integrity of information resources, equipment, systems, and facilities

    e. Legally obtains, stores, and disseminates text, data, images, or sounds

    f. Demonstrates an understanding of what constitutes plagiarism and does not represent work attributable to others as his/her own

    g. Demonstrates an understanding of institutional policies related to human subjects research

3. The information-literate student acknowledges the use of information sources in communicating the product or performance.

Outcomes Include

    a. Selects an appropriate documentation style and uses it consistently to cite sources

    b. Posts permission granted notices, as needed, for copyrighted material

For more complete information, please go to www.acrl.org/ala/mgrps/divs/acrl/standards/ informationliteracycompetency.cfm and www.ala.org/ala/mgrps/divs/acrl/issues/infolit.

Contributors

Kate Cheromcha is the hospital librarian at the Florence Grant Health Science Library, Windham Hospital, Willimantic, Connecticut.

Amanda K. Izenstark is an assistant professor in the public services department at the Robert L. Carothers Library at the University of Rhode Island, Kingston, where she serves as the reference and instructional design librarian. She is an active member of ALA and ACRL and provides research assistance to college students in the Orphan Foundation of America.

Jim Kinnie is an associate professor in the public services department at the Robert L. Carothers Library at the University of Rhode Island, Kingston, where he serves as the humanities librarian. He is an active member of ALA, ACRL, ACRL New England Chapter, and the Rhode Island Library Association.

Peter J. Larsen is an associate professor in the public services department at the Robert L. Carothers Library at the University of Rhode Island, Kingston, where he serves as the engineering and physical sciences librarian.

Members of the Instruction Unit at the University of Rhode Island, including Mary MacDonald, Amanda K. Izenstark, Jim Kinnie, Peter J. Larsen and Kate Cheromcha, won the ACRL Instruction Section Innovation Award in 2006 for their "Issues of the Information Age" public forum series.

Index

You may also be interested in

Reflective Teaching, Effective Learning: Instructional Literacy for Library Educators: This much-needed book introduces accessible concepts in instructional design (ID) and instructional technology (IT) that will help librarians at any level of experience.

Web-Based Instruction: A Guide for Libraries, Third Edition: Librarians facing the challenge of creating a Web-based project will find easy-to-understand guidance to create an educational and interactive Web site—from start to finish.

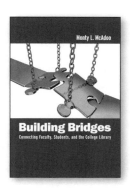

Building Bridges: Connecting Faculty, Students, and the College Library: Packed with useful tips and techniques, this handy guide offers advice on working with both students and instructors to develop successful assignments that integrate your library's resources.

Marketing Today's Academic Library: A Bold New Approach to Communicating with Students: Brian Mathews uses his vast experience to propose new visions and ideas for matching services with student needs, challenging the traditional way of thinking and providing a framework to target users more precisely.